TRANSITION DECISIONS

HOW TO GET UNSTUCK,
EMBRACE CHANGE, AND
MAKE YOUR NEXT MOVE
NOW

SHAUN
DOUGLAS
MARSHALL

"Everyone goes through transitions. You're probably going through one right now! Often these seasons of change seem to happen to us, and it feels like all we can do is try to make it through. In these pages, Shaun Marshall is our wise guide to a better way. He invites us to be active participants as we listen for God's voice during the transitions. Rather than running from change or surrendering to it, Shaun gives us a vision for welcoming our transitions, knowing God works all things—even the unexpected transitions—for our good."

—*David W. Swanson, Pastor and Author of Rediscipling the White Church*

"As I read *Transition Decisions*, my mind recalled the many moments in my life where Shaun Marshall personally guided me through change and helped me make the right transition decisions. Shaun has been a friend, ministry partner, and prayer partner for over 20 years. Thanks to his wisdom, I have transitioned from being stuck to living my best life now…and so will you!"

—*C Terrell Wheat, Author of The Innovative Prayer Leader*

Copyright © 2021 by Shaun Douglas Marshall

Published by Valiant Publishing

All rights reserved. No portion of this book may be reproduced, stored in a retrieval system, or transmitted in any form or by any means—electronic, mechanical, photocopy, recording, scanning, or other—except for brief quotations in critical reviews or articles, without prior written permission of the author.

Scripture quotations marked CEV are from the Contemporary English Version Copyright © 1991, 1992, 1995 by American Bible Society. Used by Permission. Scripture quotations marked GW are taken from GOD'S WORD®, © 1995 God's Word to the Nations. Used by permission of God's Word Mission Society. Scripture quotations marked NASB are from the New American Standard Bible®, Copyright © 1960, 1971, 1977, 1995, 2020 by The Lockman Foundation. All rights reserved. Scripture quotations marked NLT are taken from the Holy Bible, New Living Translation, copyright © 1996, 2004, 2015 by Tyndale House Foundation. Used by permission of Tyndale House Publishers, Inc., Carol Stream, Illinois 60188. All rights reserved. Scripture quotations marked NLV are taken from the New Life Version, copyright © 1969 and 2003. Used by permission of Barbour Publishing, Inc., Uhrichsville, Ohio 44683. All rights reserved.
For foreign and subsidiary rights, contact the author.

Cover design: Sara Young

ISBN: 978-1-957368-04-7   1 2 3 4 5 6 7 8 9 10

Printed in the United States of America

"Part autobiography and part theological commentary, Shaun Marshall weaves scripture, story, and principles to make sense of the places we find ourselves in life. He challenges us gently and clearly with intent to see us move forward into what God has for us. For everyone living with a vague sense of unease, caught in an emotional and spiritual status quo, or standing at a crossroads, *Transition Decisions* is a must-read. Full of encouragement, empathy, and insight that illuminates the way forward."
—*Paul Lessard, Executive Minister of Start and Strengthen Churches at The Evangelical Covenant Church*

"We all know transition must come, but we often allow fear and complacency to deter us from fulfilling our purpose and calling, ultimately stunting our growth. In this book, Shaun Marshall masterfully highlights six transition decisions, so if you desire to grow, make the decision NOW to read this book. A must-read for anyone stuck in a season of transition."
—*Sandra Riley, Pastor, Author, and Speaker*

"This book is a must-read for anyone looking for resources to get unstuck. I have discovered many people want to improve, but very few are courageous enough to make the necessary changes. Shaun Douglas Marshall has developed a proven framework for getting unstuck and a step-by-step guide for successfully navigating the maze of change and transition so the next move is smoother."
—*D. Darrell Griffin, Pastor and Author of Navigating Pastoral Leadership in the Transition Zone*

"Wow! Shaun Marshall has written a powerful and life-changing book filled with sincere encouragement, practical strategies, and wisdom from heaven. *Transition Decisions* brilliantly addresses the mental, emotional, and spiritual dynamics of change and offers solutions that help the reader to move forward with clarity and confidence. Simply a MUST-READ for anyone feeling stuck, struggling with loss, or facing major decisions."
—*William Hudson III, Pastor, Author, and Presiding Prelate at Pilgrim Assemblies International*

"I have known Shaun Marshall for over 20 years, and it has been a joy to see him grow in his life and leadership through many different moments of transition. He has poured powerful, practical insights from those experiences into the pages of this book. If you are challenged by any kind of change, *Transition Decisions* will not only give you hope but also the wisdom necessary to make your next move."

—*James T. Meeks, Author and Pastor at Salem Baptist Church, Chicago, Illinois*

"Insightful! Thought-provoking! Practical! These are the first words that came to mind as I read Shaun Marshall's *Transition Decisions*. If you are feeling the pain or positivity of change, this book will walk with you through the tough terrain of transition, and your next transition will be your best!"

—*Jon Ferguson, Author, Pastor, and Movement Leader for NewThing*

"Many thanks to Shaun Marshall for providing such an inspiring, practical, and biblically-rooted treatise on making successful transitions! We often think about the practice of "change management" in organizations, but in *Transition Decisions*, Shaun has provided us with a very personal guide to change management, which is where it all needs to start. Prepare to be challenged and encouraged to face change head-on."

—*Mindy Caliguire, Author and President at Soul Care*

"Shaun Marshall is indeed a kingdom gem who has given his life to helping others discover who they are and uncover their gifts. It has been said that "transparency is currency." If that is true, Marshall's use of authentic stories to parallel personal truths adds exponential value to this book. He has poured himself and the wisdom he has gained from years of consulting into this work. This book is a GPS that gives turn-by-turn instructions to your destination or destiny. You won't regret taking the time to open these pages."

—*Randy Borders, Author and Pastor at Faith Harvest Church, Shelby, NC*

PREFACE/DEDICATION

It was a cold, snowy day in Chicago just after the new year in 1998, and I was the proud new owner of a 1986 Fifth Avenue edition, candy-apple red Chrysler New Yorker with gangster white walls. It was my first car, left to me when my great-grandmother, Mildred Ann Houston, passed away. This amazing gift could not have come at a better time; I was in my first year of college and needed a car badly. I remember feeling a mixture of grief and gratitude—missing my precious Grand Mildred and thankful for this timely gift.

I drove that car to visit my grandmother and her sister before my three-hour trip back to campus. They lived on the first floor of a two-flat building on Chicago's far southeast side with tenants on the second floor, and my Uncle Leo was living in the basement unit. Uncle Leo was a good man who lived a hard life. His brother was murdered when they were young, and he numbed the pain of his grief with alcohol. As a result, Uncle Leo was rarely sober, seeming to live in a constant and pervasive state of inebriation. Uncle Leo was harmless but drinking often rendered him useless.

It was Uncle Leo who was seated on the front porch when I arrived at the house, wearing a windbreaker and baseball cap in single-digit weather, watching me struggle to parallel park in the snow out front.

"You're not cold, Uncle Leo?" I asked, walking up the front steps.

"I'll be good and warm in hell," he mumbled, along with some other slurred comments as he staggered behind me into the house. I immediately knew that Uncle Leo was drunk.

After about an hour's visit, I stepped onto the front porch. Uncle Leo was seated there again, this time wearing a coat and smoking a cigarette.

"You doing OK, Uncle?"

He seemed half asleep. "I'm always all right. All right," he murmured, looking down.

"OK" I replied. "See ya later." I got into the car and started the engine. While trying to pull out of the spot, my wheels started spinning.

I tried moving forward—nothing. I put the car in reverse and moved a little bit, but not much.

This time, I put the car in drive, turned the wheel hard in the direction of the street, and hit the gas. The car lurched forward, but my wheels slipped again, and the car slid at an awkward angle into the street. I tried moving forward and reversing again, and this time I got nothing but the weird smell of rubber burning in snow.

I was stuck.

While I was trying to figure out my next move, I heard a voice outside the car.

"Hold on, Nephew!"

It was my Uncle Leo. He was walking toward the car with two shovels in one of his hands and the cigarette he was smoking in the other. I got out of the car. He gave me one of the shovels and tossed his cigarette into the snow.

"Come on, let's dig," he said firmly, looking directly at me.

I watched, a bit stunned, as Uncle Leo took his shovel and began to move the snow around my right front tire.

"You get the snow from behind your rear tire," he said, speaking more clearly than I had ever heard.

I followed his instructions. When we were done, he inspected all the tires. Satisfied, he ran back onto the porch and came back with a bag of rock salt. He salted the ground in front of and behind my rear tires.

"Now," he said, again looking at me directly. "You get back in the car, and I want you to rock the car back and forth. Put it in drive, and just tap the gas until you rock your way out."

"Yes, sir." I did as he directed, and in less than 30 seconds, my car moved forward. When I rolled down my window to thank him, he cut me off.

"Pop your trunk."

When I did, he placed one of the shovels and the salt inside and slammed it closed. He came over to the driver's side window and looked directly at me again. "Always keep salt and a shovel inside of your car, OK?"

"OK, Uncle Leo. Thank you."

"All right, Nephew." I watched him walk back up the steps and into my grandmother's unit before I drove off.

For the rest of my life, I will never forget that moment. I was stuck, not sure of what to do. Just when I was about to yield to my frustration, my drunk Uncle Leo sobered up, dug me out, and gave me the tools I needed to make sure I would never stay stuck again. He told me I needed to carry two things: a shovel and salt. Someone who had been rendered useless by his own unresolved pain and intoxication saw me struggling and gave me something practical to move me forward.

I am where I am today because of people in my life who have been used by God to shovel obstacles away from my path, salt the slippery spaces before me, and rock my life back and forth until I finally made the shifts that have carried me forward. People like my mom have carried me. Her courage and resilience have provided me with a life full of survival stories to tell. People like my wife have carried me. She has continually supported me with just the right balance of agitation, loyalty, consistency, and unconditional love that has faithfully shifted my existence ever higher into God's order. My first born, Sage, has carried me. She has shifted my heart and allowed me to access places of my soul previously unexplored as a man.

People like the late Dr. Larry Lee Sherman carried me. He took me like the apostle Paul took Barnabas and poured invaluable wisdom on life and leadership that continues to light my way. People like my many family members, friends, and mentors have carried me. They've prayed with me and consistently provided me with words of clarity, counsel, and comfort that salt the words of this book. People like my Uncle Leo carried me. He interrupted his own inebriation to offer me one of his rare moments of clarity, giving me simple, practical, and effective tools to get me unstuck. Without these characters in my life story, this book would have no meaning and serve no purpose.

This book is **BECAUSE** of them, but it is **FOR** you. It is for every person who has been stuck, waiting for someone to bring them the solutions they need to move forward.

Note that this book is for everyone. It is not just for Christians, but it is written with a Christian lens. It will explain the references to Scripture and my own personal stories of faith. Please don't allow any divergence of beliefs to deter you from the hope I wish to share with you in the pages of this book. May the words of this book be the salt that dries everything that has caused you to skid. May the clarity you receive be the shovel that clears your path.

Come on. Let's dig.

FOREWORD

I have often said that people with a desire to grow must realize that growth equals change, change equals loss, and loss equals pain. Inevitably, growth equals pain. Therefore, I contend that people remain stuck not because they don't want to embrace growth, but instead, they don't know how to embrace change.

In my book, *Leadership Pain: The Classroom for Growth*, I talk about the concept of liminal space. In psychology (and theology), liminal space describes the intermediate, in-between, and transitional state. This is the space where you realize you cannot go back to where you were because a threshold has been crossed. You have yet to arrive at where you are going because it is not yet available to you.

Many people today find themselves in liminal space. This is the space between where they are and where they want, hope, or need to be. The problem is that often, critical decisions are needed in order to break free from this space and move forward.

It is for this reason I am elated for this incredible book by Pastor Shaun Marshall. I have known Shaun Marshall for over 20 years, and in that time, I have found him to be a man of integrity and a creative leader who thinks futuristically. As a consultant, I have watched many other high-capacity leaders count on him for the strategic insight to help them navigate the treacherous terrain of the in-between. As a pastor, he has passionately shepherded people to not only discover God's plan for their lives but also discern appropriate responses. The pages of this book have captured both his strategic mind as well as his pastoral heart. He writes with the kind of practical wisdom, clarity, and compassion that will make a real difference in the life of the reader, no matter what transitions you may be facing.

Please note this book is dangerous. If you don't actually want real life change, this book is NOT for you. It will not give cumbersome theory, rhetoric, or religious clichés. It will neither further enable your passive mental assent to change, nor will it allow you to continue operating from a "someday" schema. Though you will be encouraged, this book is not exclusively inspirational. This book will anger you as it disrupts your comfort zones. It will eradicate the excuses that have enabled your mediocrity. It will cause you to have conversations that force you into accountability. It will give you a clarity about your life that will prompt you to hunger for the life you have yet to live.

Simply put, this is one of the most important books you will ever read.

—Sam Chand
Friend of Shaun Marshall

CONTENTS

Introduction..15

CHAPTER 1. Decide to LEAVE 25

CHAPTER 2. Decide to LEARN 43

CHAPTER 3. Decide to BE 55

CHAPTER 4. Decide to SHIFT............................67

CHAPTER 5. Decide to TRUST 85

CHAPTER 6. Decide to TELL............................127

INTRODUCTION

Early in the morning Joshua rose and set out from Shittim with all the Israelites, and they came to the Jordan. They camped there before crossing over. At the end of three days the officers went through the camp and commanded the people, "When you see the ark of the covenant of the Lord *your God being carried by the Levitical priests, then you shall set out from your place. Follow it, <u>so that you may know the way you should go, for you have not passed this way before</u> ..."*
—Joshua 3:1-4 (NLT)

Change Happens

My late grandmother, Edwina Marshall, grew up in the Deep South. Momma survived abuse, Jim Crow, the Civil Rights Movement, and many other traumatic experiences I never heard her articulate. She was a complex woman, but she had a very simple way of imparting the wisdom she had collected through her varied life experiences. Using few words and funny phrases, she would offer priceless gems of timeless truth.

If she saw a couple she considered to be oddly matched, she would say, "There's not a pot too crooked that a lid won't fit."

If you were about to take an unwise risk, Momma would say, "A bird in the hand is worth more than two in the bush."

If you asked her how she was feeling, she would give you one of a few responses:

"Fair to midlin'."

"I do fine for a young old woman."

"I'm kickin', just not that high."

If she gave you advice you failed to heed, she would make sure to say, "I told you so," but in her own way. "I keep telling y'all … 99 percent of the time, I'm right."

Before entering the sixth grade, I transferred to a new school. I had a new schedule and new teachers. I had to learn how to navigate a new building and make new friends. I remember being deeply uncomfortable those first few days, worrying about how I would be accepted. I was feeling tremendous loss, disorientation, and uncertainty. Momma noticed the sadness on my face one morning during breakfast.

"Baby, you OK?"

I replied, "Yes ma'am. I just don't like change."

Momma looked back at me; her eyes filled with compassion. "Change don't care."

I stared at her for a moment, trying hard not to reply with anything that might earn time or punishment.

She sighed, "There are only two constants in this world: God and change. And you'd better learn how to work with both of them because change happens, and it does what it wants, when it wants, how it wants."

For 30 years, this wisdom has worked in the background of my mind, almost like a tape, replaying my grandmother's voice on a low volume every time I experience life change.

Change Happens

Change is an undeniable, unshakeable reality.

Change is a force that simultaneously functions in tandem with and untethered from our decisions.

Change can do whatever it wants. Change can happen whenever it wants. Change can happen however it wants. It doesn't require our permission.

Change rarely negotiates.

Change comes inevitably, and change inevitably changes us.

Sometimes, change comes to us as a welcome and long-awaited turn in what may have been an uncomfortable, frustrating, or lackluster season of life. For example, it may come when you finally get promoted after years of faithfulness on the job, when you get married after a period of longing for love and companionship, or when a doctor reports you are cancer-free. In these moments, change is a friend that ushers in new and more preferable realities.

There are, however, moments when change is not so kind. A car accident, receiving a layoff notice after years of faithfulness on the job, a once happy marriage ending in divorce, or the unexpected death of a loved one can take a toll on a person.

Depending upon the agent, this can be exciting, encouraging, or exhausting. You may be brimming with enthusiasm about the possibilities that lie ahead or brewing with anxiety about the dangers unknown. You may be more than ready to embrace a new reality, or you may be upset that the reality you enjoyed is changing. Whatever the case may be, you are facing a moment you haven't seen before.

In Acts 2, we see the early church in a pivotal moment of change. Prior to this, we know Jesus had risen from the dead, and before He left, He released the presence and power of the Holy Spirit to the early gathering of believers assembled together in prayer in the Upper Room. After this, Peter preached his first sermon, and this gathering of the faithful became a megachurch on its first day. Everything was great. The church kept growing. Miracles were happening. Everyone in Jerusalem was happy.

By Acts 8, the church had experienced a change they did not want or expect. Stephen, one of the first seven deacons of the church, had just been killed for boldly declaring his faith. The Bible says Saul, who will later become the apostle Paul, was consenting to his death. Not only that, but Saul was leading the charge to arrest and imprison anyone who declared faith in the Lord Jesus.

And just like that, the church found itself in what is possibly its most painful, uncomfortable, and disturbing moment since the Crucifixion. Once more, the church found itself in a dark moment in the middle. Everything was going fine, and suddenly, they experienced an "and then this happened" moment.

Have you ever been living life, minding your own business, and you looked up one day and this happened?

Happily married, and one day, DIVORCE happens.

Living in your dream home, and one day, FORECLOSURE happens.

Faithful to your career, and one day, TERMINATION happens.

Enjoying your life, and one day, A MEDICAL DIAGNOSIS happens.

Grateful for your relationships, and one day, A SUDDEN DEATH happens.

Change happens whether we plan it, expect it, or want it. Change often brings situations and circumstances we don't want, can't avoid, and can't prepare for. Often, change happens whether it has our permission or not. Most of us have never gotten a call saying, "Hey, it's Death. I'm thinking about taking your loved one on Tuesday at about 1:30. Is that a good time, or should I reschedule?" That doesn't happen because change does what it wants to do. Change wrecks us so often, and asks our permission so rarely, that we might think of change as something to be avoided.

Change Happens, But Change is Not the Problem

I often remember those words to my grandmother that fateful morning: *I don't like change.* Over the course of my life, I've come to understand that this isn't always true for me—and probably not so true for you either.

I've never hated the change of an unexpected raise. I've never known people to be frustrated with their boss because they were promoted unexpectedly or plaintive when they received the change of a marriage proposal, an expensive gift, or special recognition. One of the most significant moments of change was the day my daughter was born, and yet, becoming a father has been one of the most wonderful changes I have ever experienced. The fact is that all change isn't bad, so it's not accurate for anyone to claim that he or she doesn't like change. In fact, some change is badly needed and desired.

Change is Not the Problem

As a pastor, I once led an aging church in the process of discerning the types of changes needed in the church to create long-range sustainability for its future. The church recognized that it needed renewal if it was to have a meaningful and sustainable future. I presented the church with a comprehensive vision that involved some key changes: a facility purchase and renovation, strategic ministry to youth and young adults, renewal of discipleship ministries, and a capital campaign. The congregation embraced that vision and my ideas for change almost unanimously. However, to my surprise, as we began to work our way through the reality of those changes, many of the same people who had initially supported that vision would later work to sabotage it. This drove me nuts! We ultimately paused our planning and went back into prayer and discernment. The conclusion I first reached was that the church was in denial. *They're just a bunch of stuffy curmudgeons who hate change!*

What I eventually came to understand was that the problem wasn't the vision. It wasn't stuffy church people or their ability to understand the need for change. The problem was we had not done the deeper, longer, more difficult work of preparing ourselves to make the decisions that would need to be made as the vision moved forward. The congregation was neither mentally or emotionally prepared to know how to respond as the changes unfolded, nor was I mentally or emotionally prepared to guide them through those changes as their leader. As a result, the process of change forced everyone into a state of anxiety where they began to see the very vision that they had affirmed as the enemy. They began to fight passionately against ideas they had once welcomed enthusiastically, and for a moment, we became stuck.

On a personal level, I have experienced many different types of changes on multiple levels: job changes, relationship changes, relocations, grief and loss, and changes in my health, my finances, and my family. No matter the type of change, when I lacked the clarity necessary to make decisions that allowed me to continue moving forward in a positive direction, I became stuck.

When Have You Found Yourself Stuck?

Some of us are stuck emotionally because we have not transitioned from the change of an unexpected death.

Some of us are stuck professionally because we still don't understand why we were let go.

Some of us are stuck relationally because we have not reconciled the changes we experienced in a previous relationship, and the emotional residue from those experiences continues to keep us from moving forward.

Many of us have experienced changes that leave us stuck because as we experienced those changes, we reached a point in the process where we simply didn't know what to do.

To be clear, I believe there are two kinds of "stuck." One kind of stuck is when you CANNOT move forward. The challenge here is *immobility*. A different, more frustrating type of stuck is when you COULD move forward, but you don't quite KNOW HOW to move forward. The challenge there is *uncertainty*. Sometimes, it is both. I experienced immobility when I transferred to that new school in the 6th grade. I had no idea how to make friends or how to be accepted. I had to find new ways of existing. I felt like I had been completely upended from my life.

On the other hand, I experienced the change of uncertainty when I knew I would be experiencing a change in my career, and shortly thereafter, was presented with several job opportunities. I COULD have moved forward with any of those options, but which one was the best? Which pathway would be best for my personal growth? Best for my marriage? Best for my children?

As I tried to understand how the church I served had become stuck, and tried to process the pain I've experienced many times in my life when changes seemed to grind my forward movement to a halt, I came across the writings of the late Dr. William Bridges, an author and consultant. The following quote struck me in particular:

> "It's not the changes that do you in, it's the transitions. Change is not the same as transition. Change is situational: the new site,

the new boss, the new team roles, the new policy. Transition is the psychological process people go through to come to terms with the new situation. Change is external, transition is internal."
—William Bridges, *Transitions: Making Sense of Life's Changes*

Sometimes, the most frustrating thing about change is not that change has happened to us, but rather that we do not know how to respond. This paradox perfectly illustrates the difference between change and *transition*.

We tend to use the words change and transition interchangeably, but there is a subtle difference. Changes are unplanned and unexpected, and sometimes they are anticipated and even welcomed. In every case, the changes we remember more painfully tend to be the ones when we didn't know how to respond. No matter how big or small, expected or unexpected, joyful or painful the change, when we know what to do, we are able to move through change and experience **TRANSITION**.

Change is what happens, but transition is how we RESPOND.

Change is not always within our power. Transition is our responsibility.

Change can be an accident. Transition is a decision.

Change can be coincidental. Transition is intentional.

Change can be an event. Transition is a process.

In order to avoid getting stuck in the process of transition, we have to gain the wisdom necessary to know how and what decisions need to be made.

Transition Decisions

As a kid, my favorite book was any story from a series called *Choose Your Own Adventure*. A common feature of these books is the writer has actually taken defined characters and devised several possible storylines in the same book that play out differently, depending upon the choices made by the reader. The reader makes the choices, but the author has pre-written the characters and predetermined the outcomes of every choice.

When you come to certain pages, there is a conflict, and the conflict is resolved by your choice. If you choose to take a certain action, that choice will lead you to a different page. In this way, you could make choices that produce a different story every time you read the book.

Sometimes, the outcomes of your choices are not favorable. I distinctly remember turning to the page number that corresponded with my choice, only to find that the story had come to an unexpected and painful turn or even a sudden ending. Whenever this happened, I would go back to the previous set of choices and choose differently, which would change the storyline, ultimately leading me to a different outcome. Sometimes, I would cheat. I would turn the pages to examine the outcome of either choice and make the choices that lined up with the storyline I preferred.

Wouldn't it be nice to have these kinds of options in real life? But we do not. We painfully realize the weight of our decision-making in tandem with God's sovereignty. As a function of His omniscience, God (the Author and Finisher of our faith) knows the outcome of every decision we will make. As a function of His grace, God provides us with opportunities to discern which choices will lead us to the life which He intends for us. God does not force a path upon us, but there are more ideal pathways that He has in mind for us. Our decision-making is what allows us to experience His highest and best for our lives.

Just as in those *Choose Your Own Adventure* books, in moments of transition, we can make decisions that allow all sorts of pathways to unfold. If we want to get better at embracing change and continuing to move forward, we need to get better at making wise moves when (not if) change happens. While each book in the series features different characters, events, and storylines, the process of decision-making is often similar. It requires the ability to understand the characters, analyze each situation, think about how you would like to see each character resolve the conflict presented, and make a decision.

Have you ever met a very intelligent person who still made poor choices? This is a person who seems to know something about everything, and yet, his or her life illustrates that having information does not necessarily equate to having wisdom. Wisdom is the capacity to properly comprehend the information that you have. You can have an abundance of information and lack basic comprehension. More information with less comprehension produces overeducated failures. Wisdom gives you the ability to properly sort and comprehend information, reach accurate conclusions, and make better decisions. People aren't brilliant because of what they know. What makes them brilliant is what they are able to do with what they know. Behind every great decision is great wisdom.

There will be many different characters reading this book experiencing many different types of changes which have unfolded all sorts of pathways. Each change scenario may be radically different in its nature, but in much the same way as a *Choose Your Own Adventure* story, I believe that the process of making decisions in transition is similar in almost every case. The pages that follow are meant to guide the reader on a journey through decision points I believe to be common in every transition process and provide insight for how to make decisions that will help people get unstuck, embrace change, and make their next move. My hope is that after you read this book, you will have less desire to return to the previous pages of your life, but instead possess the confidence to respond to any change you may experience with decisions that move your life forward.

CHAPTER 1:
DECIDE TO LEAVE

Transition always starts with an ending. To become something else, you have to stop being what you are now; to start doing things a new way, you have to end the way you are doing them now; and to develop a new attitude or outlook, you have to let go of the old.
—William Bridges, *Transitions: Making Sense of Life's Changes*

"We can't stay here."

My family lived for years in a two-bedroom townhome on Chicago's far south side. Nine people lived in this house with the basement and attic converted into sleeping rooms. My grandmother had her own room, my aunt and her son shared the other room, my uncle lived in the basement, and me, my mother, and three younger brothers occupied the attic. I didn't understand this was a function of limited resources. This was the way we had always lived, and I assumed it was normal.

This reality often created tensions. There were arguments over finances or one bill or another being past due with the lights, gas, or phone being in danger of getting shut off. My grandmother was retired, and every adult in the house worked, but the resources just never seemed to be enough. One of my relatives also battled a drug addiction which often led to money and items being stolen. The stress and anxiety in our house created a situation where every moment of peace was enjoyed on a slim thread, and whenever a stressor pressed that thread, arguments would ensue, sometimes becoming physically violent.

One late night, I was upstairs in the attic playing with my younger brothers before bed when suddenly I heard violent screams and arguing. After a few moments of back and forth, my mother entered the attic, her eyes red and streaming hot tears that she immediately wiped away. There was an expression on her face I had never seen before—one that is forever etched in my memory.

"Pack a bag, and help me get your brothers ready. *We can't stay here.*"

I knew better than to ask a question. There was a sense of urgency and resolve that demonstrated arguing was unwise. I immediately began to pack a bag with everything I thought I might need; then I helped my brothers get dressed and ready.

A short time later, we left.

I don't remember the exact time, but it was late, somewhere past our normal bedtime. We exited the house and entered the night. We had our jackets, but it wasn't a very cool summer's night. We walked about seven or eight blocks and arrived at a police station. My mother had me sit in the waiting area with my three brothers, one of whom was a year and a half younger than me, another who was about 14 months old, and my youngest brother, an infant, whom I held in my arms as he slept. I am not exactly sure of the conversation my mother had with the officer at the desk. I only remember waking up after about what had to have been several hours past midnight to my mother's voice telling me that "the van" was here. I had no idea what van this was or where we were going. I just knew we weren't staying *there* anymore.

The Human Services van carried us to a small storefront church. We exited the van and went to the door. When we entered, the short, stocky pastor (who was extremely gracious given the hour) led us downstairs to the basement where a single mattress lay in the center of the floor.

Exhausted, my three younger brothers, my mother, and I laid down on that mattress and fell asleep. The next morning, we were awakened by the noise of people stepping around us to get in line to receive free groceries from the food pantry. Later that day, another van came to take us to a family shelter where we would stay for a little over a month. Eventually, the shelter worked with my mother to help her secure an apartment.

I will never forget that night. Even though I was only about ten years old at the time, I remember exactly how I felt. I didn't really feel fear. At no point during the entire ordeal did my mother allow us to feel unsafe or worried about what might happen next. I can just remember watching her and trying to understand what SHE was thinking and feeling. Lodged in my memory forever is the fact that even though she had no idea where we were going, she made sure we KEPT GOING.

My mother had directed us to leave a place we'd always known to be safe, comfortable, and reassuring and embrace a series of unknowns. There was a host of questions I never voiced in the moment: *Where are we going? How long will we be there? Will we be OK? Will we ever come home again? Will life ever be the same?*

In life, there will come moments when change happens, and you realize that you have more questions than answers. It will be in moments when you realize you will wake up tomorrow and nothing will be as you expected it the day before. It will be when you have to go places you've never been. It will be when you wonder if things will ever "return to normal." There are moments when the reality finally begins to sink in that you can no longer remain where you are, how you are, or even WHO YOU ARE, because something in your reality has changed with or without your influence. Your old reality cannot be found, and your new reality demands a response.

For my mother, this moment provided the REALIZATION and the RESOLVE necessary to do the unthinkable: carry her four children off into the dark streets of Chicago, with no certainty of where we were headed, but with full clarity that we could not remain where we were. A new reality materialized, and my mother concluded this new reality was less than preferable for herself and her four young boys. With this conclusion, she understood this new reality demanded a response, and the response would only move forward with a decision: *We can't stay here.*

In Genesis 12, we meet a Bible character by the name of Abram. Abram is a good man who seems to have a decent life going for him. One day, while minding his own business, living the life he knew, Abram received a word from the Lord: Get up and go to a land I will show you.

Whenever I read this text, and most Bible stories, I try to gather context by taking the viewpoint of the characters. In this case, I am Abram, who was presumably content with his life, making the best of things. It is in this space that I (Abram) receive a word from the Lord: Get up and go. Now, if I were Abram, my mind immediately begins racing with questions:

Why do I have to leave? Why now?

Why do I have to leave my family? Why can't they come with me?

Wait a minute ... go to a land where I will show you? How am I going to get there when I don't even know where "there" is?

When will God make more sense out of this? Will life ever be the same?

There might be more questions than these, but there may be fewer answers. Immediately, the lack of clarity leads me to the very familiar feeling of being stuck. I want to be able to make a move, but I don't know if I have enough information to make the RIGHT move.

I want to obey God, but what if I make a mistake?

I want to maximize this new opportunity, but what should I do next?

I know things are about to change, but I like my current reality. What am I going to be able to keep? What will I get in exchange for what I might lose?

I know things are different now, but why can't I just have more time to think and plan?

For most of us, a lack of clarity tends to cause immobility. We become paralyzed by the fear that arises from the absence of information, and depending upon the agent that ushers change into our lives, we become stuck in our emotional responses to what has happened. Fear, anxiety, grief, frustration, and disappointment render us immobile. If I were Abram, the book of Genesis might have had a few more chapters sharing the thoughts, emotions, complaints, and questions that have caused me to be stuck.

But you and I are not Abram. We don't know what questions ran through his mind or what feelings he felt. We don't quite know how all of his loved ones responded to the word he received from the Lord. We do know there is no evidence that Abram became stuck. In the very next verse, the Bible says Abram simply got up and went.

What made his story so different from our norm? When the call of God came to introduce him to changes that were unfolding a new reality for his life, his first recorded response was a decision: "I CAN'T STAY HERE."

It was the decision to embrace the new reality that enabled Abram to leave everything safe, comfortable, and familiar and move toward a yet undeclared destination.

In moments of change, we are often paralyzed by what we don't know. I have learned from Abram and my mother a critical piece of wisdom that enabled them both to embrace change and move forward: Every moment of change demands of us a decision, and if the result will be forward movement, then the decision must be *"I can't stay here."*

Abram was prompted by the voice of God to consider a new reality for his life. He does not appear to dwell on the unknowns. His response does not lead us to believe that he allowed himself to be stalled by questions, conversations, or complaints. Genesis 12:4 leads us to believe that Abram's pilgrimage began with an intentional decision to leave.

Three things can help us to make the decision to leave:

1) Acknowledge the prompting
2) Accept the change
3) Abandon the familiar

Change happens with or without us. *Transition requires the ability to navigate change in order to achieve a desirable future.* At some point, transition requires action, and to respond with the correct action, we must accurately discern, acknowledge, and interpret the promptings.

A prompting is a sign that communicates to us an action will soon be required. Traffic lights are promptings to let us know whether we should stop, go, or proceed with caution. Seatbelt lights on airplanes are promptings to let us know the plane is about to experience turbulence, and action is required in order to remain safe while in flight. Alarm clocks make sounds that prompt us to wake up and begin our day. Without promptings, we might miss the opportunity to do the things required of us in order to fully engage what can happen next. When we ignore the prompting of traffic lights, we cause accidents. When we ignore the prompting of the fasten seatbelt sign on airplanes, we might injure ourselves or others in the unpredictability of turbulence. When we ignore the prompting of alarm clocks, we might oversleep, miss appointments, or be unprepared for said appointments when we arrive.

Many of us miss the opportunity to transition because we fail to acknowledge the promptings. The promptings of change can be external as well as internal. An example of an external prompting is when you learn your job will be downsized due to budget cuts. An example of an internal prompting is when you arrive at work one day, and you feel a sense of contempt for your job you've never felt before. Your spirit is communicating to you that something within you has shifted, and action will be required soon.

For my mother, the stress, anxiety, and instability of our environment and all of its dynamics culminated in an event that helped to create a moment of clarity. She understood that the escalation of violence was a prompting to let her know our reality had changed. She understood we were no longer safe. My mother acknowledged the promptings, and those promptings helped her make the decisions necessary to transition us from an unsafe situation into a healthier situation.

Accept the Change

As stated before, some unexpected changes are easy to accept. I know very few people who have ever complained about a raise or promotion! However, there are types of changes that are unplanned and unwelcome.

In 1998, my grandmother was diagnosed with multiple myeloma. It is a type of cancer rarely diagnosed in black women. When given the diagnosis, she came home from the doctor and gathered the family together to explain it to us.

"Are they sure?" someone asked.

My grandmother nodded. "They're sure. This was the second opinion."

"What's the treatment?" someone else asked.

"No radiation. But I will need to start chemo soon."

No one wanted to ask the next question, but my grandmother knew. "They said two years. But the Lord has the last say."

Everyone nodded. We were unsatisfied but reassured.

After a moment, I let out the final questions: "Why? Why you? Why now?"

With tears in her eyes but strength in her voice, my grandmother replied, "Why not me? It is what it is. Only way you'll leave this world is from your deathbed. When it's my time, it will be my time. Until then, I'm gonna live. And when the time comes, I'll be ready."

With that, my grandmother stood up, went into the kitchen, and made one of the best dinners of my memory. She would later begin treatment and enjoyed three years in remission and relatively good health. We made more memories, and she passed away four years later. God did have the final say. From diagnosis to homecoming, she lived every moment to the fullest, made many more memories, laughed, cried, and experienced all of the normal emotions of a person letting go. Though the diagnosis was not what any of us wanted, she accepted it and moved forward.

Many of us are stuck because we refuse to accept the change that has come to us. We are not willing to let go of our familiar reality. We do not want to grieve our losses. We cannot even try to figure out next steps. We try to avoid grappling with the truth that the trajectory of our future has been altered against our will. The dynamic this creates within us is that we somehow form a quiet psychological resistance. We subconsciously begin to think if we deny the change, it will somehow relent, and the forces seeking to alter our reality will wave a white flag of surrender.

It is important for us to understand, however, that our unwillingness to accept change will do nothing to reverse it. Failing to accept change will not lengthen the realities we hope to keep, but it will threaten the opportunities we have left.

Grief and lament are not popular concepts because the notion of suffering is not one that our culture is willing to accept as a standard of living. Even in church, we are taught the believer is supposed to be happy; therefore, we sing happy songs while ignoring the fact many of the writings in the book of Psalms, an ancient hymnal with lyrics often set to music, were actually laments written by people expressing their grief, sadness, and sorrow. This includes Biblical hero David, as he experienced the painful transition of running from King Saul's jealous and murderous rage to leading God's holy people. In Psalm 13, David first asked God how long he must suffer and wondered when he would have the upper hand over his enemies. However, by the end of the psalm, he proclaimed his trust in God's unfailing love for him. David knew grief and crying out to God were essential to embracing change and the troubles he faced. However, he also fully understood God was not forsaking him and had a much greater plan than David could have imagined.

While my grandmother never pretended to like this change, she *accepted* it. While she did grieve and mourn, she had very few pity parties. She was a strong woman who had learned how to accept the unacceptable, adjust, and move forward. And because she was able to accept that this disease would change her life, she was able to enjoy the life she had left to live.

Most transitions require us to *name and accept* loss. Something must be left. Before we can advance in life, we must accept loss. Unfortunately, we are not generally taught how to grieve well. We therefore tend to resist the acceptance of loss, making this one of the most difficult aspects of the transition process.

I belong to an informal network and community of ministers, some of whom I have experienced life with for over 20 years. I am blessed to say in a world where there seem to be more and more people in ministry that prey on the vulnerable, these relationships afford me with a safe space of authenticity and accountability. The hard truth our group has acknowledged is that much of what we know as preaching today is commercial entertainment. Many false preachers work hard to get churchgoers excited about spiritual promises without helping them reconcile psychological pain. Often when we come to church, the songs we sing in worship are happy, positive, and primarily ego-centered. We don't really teach songs that give people an opportunity to work with the difficulties of life. Most liturgies revolve around self-centered and consumeristic ideas: "God's gonna do it. God's gonna fix it. It's gonna be alright." Sometimes, life is not alright. In fact, sometimes it's all wrong. And my circle of ministers can confess often we program people to think if they just confess it, name it, and claim it, a wonderful experience will magically appear. This produces a dissociated discipleship that robs people of the ability to handle pain and loss in any healthy way.

Here is the reality: In life, we will struggle with loss and grief because change of any kind will bring it. Before you can transition through change, you must learn to transform the pain those changes have caused you. Simply put, you have to mourn before you can move.

In Acts 7, Stephen, a prominent Christian believer, takes the Jewish leaders to task as he proclaims God's truths and accuses them of killing the Messiah. He speaks eloquently to his own peril as he is then stoned to death with the approval of Saul. This changes things for the early church as the persecution of believers grows, threatening their mission and their lives.

The church had to mourn Stephen. Stephen was a good man—the Bible describes him as a man of faith, filled with the Holy Spirit. And he died doing exactly what was pleasing to the Lord. Sometimes in life, we have to grieve good things that God sent to us, simply because those things and people can't move forward with us. Stephen was good in every way, but his time was done, and his death would result in a scattering of the apostles. Stephen's death and the scattering would bring about a spreading of the gospel on an epic scale. The early church had to lament Stephen's death but also had to turn to see what God would bring next.

Many of us are stuck because we lost something good. We're still trying to hold onto that, and we're unable to see what God wants to bless us with next.

This is often the toughest reality to grasp because we have no power over what we lose. I think we believe if we resist grief, we can somehow deny the power of loss. As a result, many of us have unconsciously moved from change to change in life carrying a string of losses we have never really grieved. We have not mourned what we've lost in our past, which keeps us from doing the things in the present that will allow us to pursue the future God has promised. Many of us never fully maximize our potential and transition into our purpose because we are unwilling to process our pain. In order to receive what God wants to do next, we have to be willing to release the pain we carry over the things we have lost that we did not want to lose.

I pastored my first church for nearly four years. In those four years, I officiated over 30 funerals. The second funeral I did was for someone who had become one of my favorite members, a woman named Betty. Ms. Betty was one of my most faithful members. Betty sang in the choir and was a passionate worshiper. She was also a prayer warrior who loved my wife and me. On many Sundays after the worship service, Betty would regularly give me a hug and remind me, "Pastor, I love you and your wife. You are my family." Then she would pat the weapon hiding in her purse and add, "Remember, if anyone bothers you, I've got your back."

One day, Betty went to the emergency room complaining of a pain in her side. God called Betty home that day.

When they brought her body into the church before the funeral, I stood over her casket, and I said, "Now, Lord, if you just needed to take someone, I had some other members to recommend. Why'd you have to take this one?"

But I had to accept it.

Grief begins with accepting your loss, and after you accept it, to name your feelings and lead your feelings forward.

Because my grandmother was strong enough to accept a change she did not want, we were able to celebrate the blessing her life was to us more intentionally. Though the early church was grieved by what happened to Stephen and the disruption it caused, they were able to grieve, but they continued to spread the Good News wherever they went. Due to Betty's faith and spirit of worship, I can express grief at her loss but joy in her homecoming.

Abandon the Familiar

> "You can't follow the thread of your life very far before you find "the past" changing. Things that you haven't remembered in years reappear, and things that you've always thought were so turn out to be not so at all. If the past isn't the way you thought it was, then the present isn't, either. Letting go of that present may make it easier to conceive of a new future."
> —William Bridges, *Transitions: Making Sense of Life's Changes*

Simply put, you will never lay hold of "next" until you let go of "now."

The problem for many of us is we are delaying our transition *by attempting to negotiate with next about how much now we can take with us.* We try to hold on to now until we know we can trust next, so we have something to fall back on "just in case." This is why so many amazing stories of transition begin with deeply painful stories of loss. Sometimes, God has to break our hearts "here" before we can move our feet "there." Transition demands you to make the decision that *where you are can no longer be trusted*. In order to get where you must go, you must first accept you can no longer be where you are.

In the Genesis story of Abram, he had to acknowledge what would be left behind like familiarity, comfort, relationships, and expectations.

"Endings are better than beginnings, and patience is better than pride," (Ecclesiastes 7:8, NLT). Some things were not made to last. Some blessings or relationships came to serve a purpose. In our pride, we sometimes try to force things to live longer than God wants them to. This is ultimately because we think we're smarter than God, and we think what we have is better than what He might give us. Transition decisions require us to forsake the comfort of our past in order to embrace the promise of the future. Sometimes, a better tomorrow will only come when we allow a "pretty good today" to die. In this way, sometimes the greatest hindrance to experiencing the next thing God wants to do in our lives is the last thing God *did*. The children of Israel could not get excited about milk and honey because they still had a memory of fish and leeks.

Our human nature often chooses familiar pain over favorable possibilities. We will never reach the future until we have resolved to let go of the present. Letting go means taking your hands off of something you have held onto. It means loosening your grip and embracing the reality that you will no longer hold what you've held.

Before you can engage with transition, you must consider the cost. You must reconcile what you will need to let go. When we engage transition, we may need to let go of some relationships. We may need to let go of comfortable spaces. As we move forward, we let go of familiar experiences, patterns, routines, and habits we have grown accustomed to because they will no longer fit in the new reality. We let go of the illusion of control and our need for more and more of it. We let go of the need for the approval of those who may not understand or agree with our choices.

We decide to let go—to release that which we are holding onto—because whether we have all of the information or not, we have reached the conclusion there is something more compelling waiting for us to lay hands upon.

We let go of what we have lost because we are aware of things waiting to be found.

We let go of what is comfortable because we are more aware of what is possible.

We let go of what we know because we have developed more hope in the unknown.

When we let go, we are saying goodbye.

The Problem with Goodbye

My wife is what you might think of as a "social introvert." When we are entertaining or out with friends, my wife is often the one most animated and engaged in conversation. She truly delights in having time to connect with friends and loved ones, and when we have that opportunity, she is present. However, there comes a time at every engagement when my wife and I will be seated at the table in a restaurant, and I will feel a gentle pat on my knee. That is the signal from my wife she has reached the point where her social energy is spent, and she is ready to conclude the engagement. This signal provides me with the same prompting as the fasten seatbelt sign does on the airplane as it begins its descent. She has made me aware that it is time to "land" the conversation and prepare to say goodbye for the evening.

We all know what it feels like to have houseguests who, having unwittingly overstayed their welcome, miss those subtle, passive-aggressive cues: "My goodness, look at the time. I had no idea it was this late!" or "You guys have a long drive home, don't you?" In those moments, goodbyes are welcomed. Or those awkward interactions when you bump into an ex, and you don't have very much to say to one another. These are all examples of moments we *want to* leave.

The problem with goodbye is we are often prompted to say goodbye to things we do not want to let go of, people we are emotionally unprepared to lose, and moments we never wanted to end. For this reason, it is common in our culture for us to think of goodbye as a difficult thing.

Sometimes we are forced to say goodbye. I remember sometime after learning about my grandmother's cancer, I received an early morning call from my mother: "Please hurry to the house as soon as you can."

"What's wrong?" I asked, my heart racing, trying to prepare myself for what I was already afraid to hear.

"Just get to Momma's house as soon as you can."

I hopped in the car and raced to her house at top speed, my thoughts and emotions flying even faster. I knew her cancer had returned, and she was looking more and more frail, but I was not ready for this news.

When I arrived at the house, my mother opened the door, and everyone was seated in the living room in a circle, including my grandmother, who was wiping tears from her eyes. The shock of seeing her alive, which quickly shifted into relief that she was alive, was immediately followed by the alarming recognition that something was still wrong. I scanned the room and saw my brothers, aunts, and uncles.

"What happened?"

The room stood still. Finally, my uncle stood up and laid a hand on my shoulder. "Doniesha was shot last night. They took her to the hospital and worked on her for hours, but she didn't make it."

My cousin, Doniesha, and I were raised like siblings. She was killed in a drive-by shooting. Wrong place, wrong time. This is not at all the goodbye I was prepared to give.

When a goodbye happens that we don't want or expect, it's hard to see the goodbye as a good thing. Just like with any goodbye, there are a few things to acknowledge. The problem with goodbye is that sometimes goodbyes remind us that our expectations for the way things should go can be unexpectedly disrupted.

Acts 1 tells us Jesus rose from the dead and presented Himself to His disciples. When they met together before His ascension, the disciples asked if now was the time Jesus would restore the Kingdom to Israel. The Jews believed that their Messiah would overthrow the Roman government and be their earthly, natural king. They believed that because Jesus had defeated death, it was a sign He now held the power to defeat Caesar. These followers clearly had an expectation for what they thought should happen next, but Jesus told them these things were "not for them to know." The problem with goodbye is it often forces us to sit with the fact there are some things about the future that are simply not for us to know or understand right away. There will be losses that don't make sense. There will be shifts and changes that come without warning. Life will seem to be heading in one direction, and suddenly, the road twists and turns, carrying us in a completely different direction.

Goodbye reminds us that life doesn't take orders from us. That's a problem if we believe we are in control of our destiny and the masters of our own fate. Goodbye painfully reminds us we are the masters of nothing except our response.

It was problematic and painful for me to let go of my beloved Doniesha at just 22 years old. But I had to say goodbye.

The Purpose of Goodbye

There are some transitions that are more welcome because they make more sense to our minds and are more easily reconciled within our emotions like promotions, graduations, and relocations, that come with new and greater career opportunities. The goodbyes that come with these transitions may still be difficult, but we more willingly embrace them because we agree with their purpose.

In his book, *Necessary Endings*, Dr. Henry Cloud says, "Getting to the next level always requires ending something, leaving it behind, and moving on. Growth itself demands that we move on. Without the ability to end things, people stay stuck, never becoming who they are meant to be, never accomplishing all that their talents and abilities should afford them."

We tend to be more welcoming to "pleasant" transitions because we understand the goodbyes that come from them are necessary for the growth we have chosen to embrace. And yet, the reality is no matter the agent of change, whether sudden or planned, pleasant or painful, welcomed or unwelcomed, every goodbye serves the same purpose: to reconcile that the time has come to *let go and move on*.

The Power of Goodbye

Goodbye is a powerful decision. It is often the key that opens the door to the journey of transition. Sometimes, the only difference between a painful change and a powerful transition is making the choice to *let go*.

Because Abram was willing to let go, a decision was made that helped to shape the most powerful narrative history will ever tell. His decision to leave his reality was the decision that created a new reality for generations to come.

Because of my mother's courage to let go, a decision was made that forced my family to confront the unhealthiness and dysfunction we had come to accept as normal. My brothers and I would later arrive in a place of safety where new norms were established. What eventually followed was healing, growth, and reconciliation. A new future was created, and we emerged a stronger family.

I am convinced this transition decision is the most difficult—but one of the most critical. When you can make the decision to leave, it frees you to do the work necessary to calculate your next steps. The rest of this book will be committed to helping you determine your course of action in transition, so you can know what hitting the water looks like.

CHAPTER 2:
DECIDE TO LEARN

Getting wisdom is the wisest thing you can do! And whatever else you do, develop good judgment.
—Proverbs 4:7 (NLT)

There are minor changes we make and changes that happen to us that do not require in-depth thinking, psychological processing, or fiery prayers. In the Midwest, when seasons change from fall to winter, we shift clothes in and out of our wardrobe without a lot of angst. We put away the sandals and dust off our boots. We hang up our swimsuits and unpack our wool coats. (Although, if you live in Chicago, you might keep both handy.) I have changed my hairstyle, my car, and my shoes many times. I've made simple job changes in my youth that did not have a lasting, dramatic impact on my career. My life was not deeply marked when I moved from my grandmother's house to a one-bedroom apartment in a mixed-income neighborhood during grad school.

But there are changes that cause us to enter transition:

When we accept a wedding proposal

When we accept a job offer that requires relocation

When we change careers

When we must file bankruptcy

When we receive the diagnosis of a serious illness

When a loved one suddenly and unexpectedly dies

Whether by choice or not, there are many varied circumstances of life change when transition becomes our reality. While each of these scenarios may be vastly different from the others, there are some aspects of transition that are common across all experiences. It is critical to learn the laws that apply so that you can engage transition in healthy ways.

A Different Set of Rules

Anyone who has learned how to drive an automobile in the United States knows the basics:

We drive on the left side of the car and the right side of the street.

The solid yellow lines in the road separate the lanes of oncoming traffic while dashed white lines separate lanes of traffic moving in the same direction.

Generally, the highway speed limit is anywhere between 55 and 70 mph.

When we follow these general guidelines, they allow us to move from here to there safely. However, when we change zones, geographies, and governments, we may find a different set of rules apply. For example, in the United Kingdom, the steering wheel sits on the *right* side of the vehicle, and drivers drive on the *left*. In Pakistan, lanes of oncoming traffic may be separated by dashed white lines, and yellow lines are used to indicate the shoulders of the road. In Germany, there are sections of the autobahn (federal highway system) that have no speed limit! Driving according to the U.S. rules of the road will generally make you a safer traveler. But following the U.S. rules of the road outside of the U.S. may cause you to have an accident or even break the law. Therefore, it is critically important we understand the rules that apply to the zone we are in.

The late Dr. William Bridges wrote and lectured extensively on transition. He created a model for transition that describes the three main phases:

Endings. Endings are the zone in which we make the decision to leave, as discussed in chapter one, because it is in this zone we acknowledge changes that have HAPPENED or changes that are NECESSARY. It is in this zone we experience the initial trauma of loss. It is in this zone we come to the definitive conclusion our current reality is not sustainable. It is in this zone we hear the unwelcomed news that our loved one has been pronounced dead. It is in this zone our divorce decree has been finalized. It is in this zone we pack up our office to leave after the company has downsized. It is in this zone we make the courageous decision to submit our resignation, accept the new position, or relocate for a new opportunity. This is the zone where grief begins.

New Beginnings. The new beginning is the ideal future state. It is the preferred reality that we long for, following either a planned or unplanned ending. When a transition is unfolding a desirable change, it has usually begun as the result of a decision to pursue a preferred new beginning.

We end our singleness in order to share life with another.

We leave one job in order to follow a career path that is more fruitful and fulfilling.

We relocate in order to find a better living situation in another place.

In these situations, our focus tends to be on the new beginning. The new beginning is always shining with hope, stirred with optimism, and best pronounces our opportunities.

When transition is the result of some unplanned and often unwelcome change, it is often because something we did not want to end has ended.

Our spouse has requested a divorce.

A loved one has died despite our prayers and petitions for their healing.

We have been laid off from a job we love.

In these situations, our emotional energy tends to be absorbed by the *ending*. We are filled with grief, stifled with sadness, and most aware of our losses. Eventually, we will long for the new beginning: a place where we will be able to abandon the pain of the unwanted change we have endured. And it is often true that our longing for the new beginning causes us to underestimate the difficulty of the neutral zone.

The Neutral Zone. The neutral zone is the middle. It is the space between the ending and the new beginning. In this space, there can be tremendous anxiety because there is significant uncertainty. The neutral zone is *disorienting*. It is a space where you are no longer where you were, but you aren't where you want to be yet. It is a space filled with unknowns, confusion, frustration, and anxiety. In the neutral zone, there is an abundance of unusual activity happening around us and within us. Another leading voice on the topic of transition is my friend and mentor, Rev. Dr. D. Darrell Griffin. He often says, "The neutral zone is the space between where we were and where we will be. It is the meantime … and the meantime is a MEAN time!"

It is during the "meantime" of the neutral zone where the decisions we make are critical not only to how the transition itself unfolds but also to how we grow (or languish) in the process. It's a place where, if we fail and don't know the "rules of the road," we can find ourselves stuck very quickly. This is by no means an exhaustive list, but here are some important "laws" we should learn that usually govern the neutral zone road when we travel through transition.

The Law of Preparation: Transition is a Process

It is important to note the decision to transition is not the transition itself.

When I'm driving on the expressway, my GPS will often warn me I will soon be approaching my exit. This does not mean I should immediately veer to the right or the left, as this will most certainly cause an accident and possibly injury. The GPS is *prompting* me to prepare for repositioning. It's letting me know now is the time to check the lanes of traffic around me for the right opportunity to change my signals, move into the correct lane, adjust my speed, and prepare for my exit.

Depending upon the uniqueness of the change dynamics you are facing, your "on ramp" to transition may be shorter or longer than for others once you have made the decision to leave. The main idea here is this: At the beginning of transition, you are *preparing* more than you are planning and anticipating more than you are acting. For example, if you are the person who has been feeling the prompting to start a business, maybe the smartest thing for you to do isn't to go in and quit your job tomorrow. Maybe what you begin to do is to evaluate where you could make a turn, formulate a plan, and develop a strategy so that when the exit comes, you'll be ready to take it when you see it.

The Law of Healing: Transition Will Bring Opportunities to Process Your Pain

Dr. Paul Brand was a well-respected surgeon who made breakthrough discoveries in medicine while working with patients suffering from leprosy. In his book, *The Gift of Pain*, he shares the story of Tanya, a four-year-old patient who had developed a rare disorder known as congenital indifference to pain, a condition similar to leprosy. Because of this condition, Tanya would develop serious injuries but experience no pain to signal that something was wrong. On the one hand, one might think it would be a gift to live free of pain. However, Dr. Brand argues the less we are able to actually feel pain, the more destructive it becomes. He suggests we think of pain not as something to be avoided, but as a "beloved enemy." When we lose the ability to feel pain, we lose the messages pain brings to us. When we avoid pain, we also avoid the wisdom pain imparts to us.

One of the challenges of transition is it requires the ability to embrace pain as a teacher. Whenever you experience a transition, you will negotiate with some form of loss. The most difficult transitions we face are the ones where the losses stir the emotions we have buried deep within our souls from losses we have not truly grieved or processed.

It doesn't matter who you are. If you breathe air, at some point in your life, you will experience some type of pain. Because transition forces you to name losses, it strikes the chords of loss you have experienced but have yet to name. When you move through transition, you must anticipate the resurfacing of old conflicts and the reopening of old wounds. There are lessons to be learned from these unresolved issues that will help you as you grow forward. For example, if you are experiencing a divorce and were the child of divorce, the pain of the childhood experience often speaks up in the current situation. Things you may not have thought about or felt in years can come crashing down in unexpected ways.

Peter Scazzero, author of *Emotionally Healthy Spirituality,* says, "Unprocessed emotions don't die, they just go somewhere else." When we refuse to acknowledge and work through sadness, anger, grief, regret, offense, etc., these feelings don't go away—they go deep within. Resting beneath our conscious mind, these emotions drive our demeanor and behavior in ways we often fail to realize. When these long-buried emotions awaken, we usually try our best to ignore and avoid them as we focus on manipulating our circumstances. It is our nature to believe if we can change the circumstances, we can somehow alleviate, or even avoid, more pain. It is important to name and confront these conflicts or feelings and spend time discerning how you are to learn and grow from them.

This is why God often allows spaces between transitions. Sometimes, when we feel like we are trapped in "limbo" or stuck in a holding pattern, it is because God, in the wisdom of His grace, is giving us a delay to deal with issues we have denied. If we allow them, our unprocessed emotions and unresolved pain will bypass our judgment and make our transition decisions for us. It is absolutely imperative we deliberately make space during transition to *face our forsaken feelings*.

The Law of Honesty: There is No Transition Without Truth

It just wasn't working.

I was a young, high-level leader at a fast-growing and prosperous church. I was being compensated very well for my role, and for a season, I was effective. I had earned the praise of my boss, the pastor, and my peers. I had an amazing job, and things were going great.

However, as the ministry grew, so did the challenges, the demands, and the conflicts. I was no longer the best person for the role—no matter how badly both my boss and I wanted me to be. There were gifts and skills that were necessary for ensuring success in the role I simply did not possess. Not only that, but the Lord had begun to stir new gifts and passions within me that I needed a different space to explore.

I checked in with my mentor, Dr. Samuel Chand, and asked if he could help me process what I was experiencing. He said, "Well, one of two things is happening. Either you're growing up, and you need to mature and recognize things won't always go your way in leadership, or God is stirring your nest, and you're moving into transition." He challenged me to pray about these ideas, which I did. After some time in prayer and reflection, I realized God was preparing me for something new and different.

Sometimes, when you're in transition, you simply learn to deal with yourself. You learn to be honest about your strengths and your deficiencies. You learn to be honest when perhaps you're in a situation where you're growing, and it's time for you to move to a new situation.

Sometimes, you have to say, "It's just not working. Maybe I'm not a good fit. Maybe I'm being challenged and called to another environment or to another setting."

When you're able to recognize that and be honest with yourself, it stops you from making other people the problem. I was in this place where I was making my boss the problem. In reality, it was simply God saying to me, "Your season is shifting. I'm calling you into transition." I was able to stop making accusations. I was able to sit in front of my boss and say, "First, I take responsibility for these areas I need to deal honestly with myself about in this role. Second, I've been in prayer, and I'm discerning maybe God is calling me to the next step." We would go on to have a great conversation, after which I transitioned out of the organization. I gained wisdom in that process that helped me to transition with honor and grace without burning any bridges.

Transition will teach you to tell yourself the truth first. How are you being challenged to grow? How are you being challenged to rethink where you are? Sometimes, the reason why we get stuck is because there is a truth God is trying to teach us about ourselves that we are unwilling to accept. It might be difficult, but as we grow more willing to name, embrace, and reconcile the truth of transition, we can receive difficult truth as the information we desperately need in order to *grow and go*. The sooner we embrace the truth, the sooner we will gain the clarity, courage, and confidence necessary for transition.

The Law of Disappointment: Transition Will Teach You to Regularly Reset Your Expectations

In the book of Exodus, Moses was called to deliver the children of Israel from Egypt and to lead them to the land of Canaan, a land that was flowing with milk and honey. But then there was this wilderness—this transition phase. This part was difficult for the children of Israel because they now had to recognize everything they left behind in Egypt. Sure, they had been slaves in Egypt, forced to work difficult situations and to make bricks without straw. But when they arrived in the wilderness, they began to complain to God and to Moses, saying, "At least when we were slaves in Egypt, we had fish and leeks." The people who had been delivered began to reminisce about how good they'd had it when they were in bondage!

There's something about transition that will cause you to even miss some situations that weren't good for you. This is because when choosing between the land of familiar bondage and the land of uncertain blessings, our minds will default to choosing the familiar. The children of Israel began to complain to God because there was no water in the desert.

It was a *desert*!

There was no water in the desert, yet God, in His mercy, chose to provide them with water from a rock, and it was just enough to keep them moving forward. We must learn what transition has to teach us about resetting our expectations. Sometimes we're offended when we move through transition because life isn't panning out the way that we planned. Transition will disrupt our thoughts and expectations about the way life should go.

In that messy, middle, neutral zone phase, where it's not the ending and it's not the beginning, and we're not where we were, but we're also not where we hope to be, we must be very careful about setting unreasonable expectations for ourselves. We would do well to hold life loosely in these moments, to resist the temptation to compare one phase of life with another. We would do well to accept our current realities in transition just as they are without overcomplicating or oversimplifying them. It may not be the end of the world, but it may truly be an uncomfortable experience. It may not be an ideal situation, but it may not be the worst-case scenario. When change happens, and life presents us with circumstances we did not expect, we would do well to learn that this is *exactly* what life does.

The Law of Separation: Transition May Cause You to Lose People You Thought You Needed

On the singing competition *The Voice*, there is something called "The Blind Audition." In the blind audition, the coaches' chairs are faced with their backs to the artist during a performance. If a coach is impressed by the performance, they press a button, which turns their chair toward the artist and illuminates the bottom of the chair to read, "I want you." At the conclusion of the performance, an artist either defaults to the one coach who turned around or selects a coach if more than one coach expresses interest. If no coach has pressed a button, the artist stands rejected and is unable to move forward in the competition.

Many of us have delayed our opportunities to transition because we have been performing for the endorsement and affirmation of others. We place our lives on hold, waiting for someone "significant" to want us. We wait to move forward in whatever God has created us to do because we're waiting for someone else to "push a button" and give us their approval. Because we have not received and internalized the validation of God, we reduce our life to a series of auditions. We step on stage, give everything we've got, and when we look up to see the backs of man still turned to us, we withdraw in defeat, waiting for the next opportunity to win someone's approval.

It is important for us to understand we don't have to spend our lives waiting for the approval of people. God has already accepted, endorsed, validated, and approved us. It doesn't mean we become loose cannons or reject the wisdom and authority of those who can make us better. What it does mean is even when all backs are turned to you, and if you never see an "I want you" sign, God's voice has already affirmed you, and you can still move forward.

In my case, the person I "lost" was a mentor and friend whom I deeply respected. Through a set of unusual circumstances involving lies, betrayal, and broken trust, a connection that had endured for more than 20 years was severed. I had never imagined a future in ministry without a connection to this person. Of course, I have since realized this was exactly the problem. Losing this mentor, though difficult, presented separation that was needed in order for me to move forward in God's call for me and my ministry.

The Law of Transformation: Change Changes You First

Most of us know that caterpillars enter into cocoons to become butterflies, but the process of transformation is quite interesting.

What starts that process is metamorphosis. Changes begin according to a developmental schedule programmed into the DNA of the caterpillar. There's something within the body of a caterpillar called imaginal discs. When it becomes time for the caterpillar to enter into metamorphosis, the imaginal discs in the caterpillar begin to spin inside of it in order to break down and change its molecular structure. Then, as a caterpillar enters its cocoon, the caterpillar's body begins to break down, those imaginal discs begin to melt the caterpillar's body until its DNA restructures, and it grows into the form of a butterfly.

For the caterpillar, it literally feels like it's dying, because in a sense, it is. The caterpillar is experiencing an intense developmental event. After this process, it will never go back to caterpillar form again, so it's got to shed its previous form in the cocoon. Then it will need to break through the cocoon in order to live in its new form. This entire process requires stamina, resolve, and resilience.

Many of us have felt the intense pressure and trauma of change. The tumult and trauma of change can leave us desperately seeking reprieve. The last thing we want after a stressful change is more change. Our prayers to God might include requests for Him to stop the onslaught of changes we are experiencing. If we feel like we're close to death in transition, though we probably are not in a literal sense, it's because that's part of the process of us being transformed in transition. *You can't change change until change changes you.*

CHAPTER 3
DECIDE TO BE

Lord, we ain't what we oughta be. We ain't what we want to be. We ain't what we gonna be. But, thank God, we ain't what we was.
—Rev. Dr. Martin Luther King, Jr., from the
1962 speech *"A Promise Unfulfilled"*

In high school, every student was required to wear a school-issued ID badge. We were required to wear these badges daily in order to gain access into the building. If you didn't have your school ID when you entered the building, then you had to wait by the door for the security staff to take you to the main office and verify your identity. They did this for a number of reasons, but the primary reason was safety. They simply wanted to verify that everyone entering the building was entering for valid purposes. I also believe they wanted to teach us the importance of making sure you're able to verify who you are when you move in and out of different situations.

One of the reasons why I believe many of us get stuck in transition is because we don't know who we really are. We come to certain turning points in life and become stuck because our identity has yet to be verified. We find ourselves many times stuck in situations because we believe that those situations are acceptable for us based upon our understanding of ourselves. Many of us have seen the movie *The Lion King*, and we know the main character of that movie, Simba, was a young lion cub who suffered the tragic experience of losing his Father, Mufasa. When Mufasa died, Simba was told to run away and never return. On his journey into the jungle, he met two animals who began to help him see himself differently. He found himself in community with those animals who weren't like him and weren't helping him to be who he'd been created to be. Meanwhile, there was a situation back home that desperately needed Simba to come back and realize who he really was. I believe that many of us are in a place in life where we're stuck, where we're held back because we've allowed ourselves to be in situations that have kept us from knowing who we really are.

If we are to successfully navigate transition, it is critically important we discover and become the version of ourselves that our future demands.

When I graduated from high school, I went away to college. College was different. It wasn't just being in a different city or adhering to a different set of expectations. A different level of maturity was required. No one was going to make sure I went to class. I had to manage my own schedule now. I was no longer a "grader." I was a freshman. The transition from high school to college meant I didn't just have to verify I was actually Shaun Marshall. This transition required me to become a different type of Shaun Marshall than I had been before.

This Transition Required Me to Transform

One of the challenges we face in transition is it demands of us to be more of something we haven't been yet. I didn't fully understand it, but throughout elementary, middle, and high school, I was being equipped with what I needed to be a different student at each level. I was being developed to operate at the college level. The skills, understanding, and responsibility that would be demanded of me as a college student were in me, but now I needed to demonstrate those abilities independently with a greater level of consistency and maturity. The previous seasons of my life had been preparing me for what was coming next.

In chapter one, we talked about the decision to leave. We learned in order to make our next move, we must be willing to let go of where we've been. In making the "decision to be," we must first realize that sometimes transition will require us to not only let go of where we've been, but who we've been.

Two Truths and a Lie

There's a classic icebreaker game called "Two Truths and a Lie." The objective of the game is to make it fun to learn two interesting things about a person while mixing those truths in with a lie. For example, here's how I would play the game:

1) I missed the chance to meet Barack Obama ... twice.
2) I have been arrested ... twice.
3) I've been hit while crossing the street by a limousine ... twice.

Of the three items above, two are true, and one is a lie. The fun of the game for the seasoned player is to make statements that are either so implausible that it would be hard to believe, while creating a lie that would be somehow plausible as a means of making it more difficult and more interesting for those guessing. The fun for participants is not only in getting to know people better by sorting through fact and fiction, but also discovering how "creative" some people can be in telling lies (by the way, I've never been arrested, and I still have flashbacks whenever I see limousines)!

Obviously, there is no fun in playing this game with people who know you well because they not only know what is true about you, they might also have a good read on when you're lying. Likewise, the game requires you to *know yourself* and your life well enough to make true statements fit together with a clever fabrication. After all, you should know you, right?

Sometimes, transition places us in situations and circumstances that make us less certain about what is most true about who we are. Sometimes, our disdain for change is actually because we have not only become comfortable with our "where" and our "what," we have become comfortable with our "who." The trouble with "comfort" is it is easy to grow comfortable with an incomplete version of who we are.

When "Doing You" No Longer Works

What happens when life brings you changes that make it difficult for you to be who you've been?

When I got married, my wife and I moved in together. It was wedded bliss. One day, I sent my wife a quick text to let her know I would be hanging out with my friends after work. We met up at church and went out to eat. Sometime during dinner, I noticed my phone battery was low, so I texted my wife to tell her that my battery was low, but I would be home "soon." As was my habit at that stage of maturity, I proceeded to sit and talk until the restaurant finally shut down well after midnight. My friends and I walked to our cars and continued to talk in the parking lot until around 2 am. When I finally arrived home around 3 am, I was shocked to find my wife was still awake.

"Where were you?"

The question caught me off guard. "I told you I was with my friends."

"Yes, but you texted me almost four hours ago to say your phone was dying, but you would be home 'soon.'"

"Oh, honey," I said, "I was fine. It was just me hanging out with the guys."

My wife rolled her eyes. "Husband, this is unacceptable. I was worried about you and had no way to communicate with you to make sure you were OK. At any rate, I'm glad you are home. Now, I can go to bed."

I was stunned and speechless. I watched my wife go to bed.

Unacceptable? I thought to myself. *You are my wife, not my mother!*

When I processed the conversation with a mentor of mine a few days later, he laughed. "Buckle up boy. That's marriage. She isn't telling you it is unacceptable for you to spend time with your friends. What she is telling you is it is unacceptable for you to be married and behave like you're still single."

That was the moment I began to understand. I was a happily married man, but I was still becoming a husband. I had embraced the transition of being married, but I was still embracing the subsequent transformation of becoming a responsible and thoughtful spouse.

Every transition presents you with an opportunity to be a different version of yourself. Simply put, every transition requires you to be. This is important because sometimes in transition, particularly early in the process, we get stuck because we simply don't know what to do. When we find ourselves in that space, where we are in transition and we don't know what to do, the best thing is to be.

> *The heavens proclaim the glory of God. The skies display his craftsmanship. Day after day they continue to speak; night after night they make him known. They speak without a sound or word; their voice is never heard. Yet their message has gone throughout the earth, and their words to all the world.*
> —Psalm 19:1-4 (NLT)

How do the heavens declare the glory of God and utter speech yet do this without having a mouth? Their declaration comes from their design. By simply being the heavens, the heavens point us to the glory and majesty of a masterful Creator. Like the heavens, our God-ordained and unique design speaks of the purposes for which we've been created to serve. It can help us gain clarity for our next move because when we realize who we *be*, we will *do* what we *be*. (It might be bad English, but it is good theology!)

Be Yourself ... Again!

What if you really haven't been you yet?

What if all of the decisions you've made so far in life have been from a place of misinformation and misunderstanding about who you truly are? What if the agent that ushered in your moment of change is not a devil coming to restrict you, but an angel coming to release and rename you?

Most Bible characters received a name change following a significant transition in their lives. When Abram established a covenant with God, the Lord changed his name to Abraham to affirm he would be a "high father" of many nations. When Jacob wrestled with the angel, the Lord changed his name from Jacob (trickster) to Israel (he who struggled with God and triumphed) to affirm God had given him his power and posture. Jesus changed Simon's name to Peter (rock) as an affirmation of the stability and strength his leadership would bring to the early church. Following their transformations, these people—ordinary people just like you and I—made incredible next moves and left powerful stories that are still being told today. One of our highest priorities in transition, then, is to focus our energy not on the outcomes, but on the becomes. Before we ask, "What's next?" we have to figure out, "Who are we anyway?"

The Right Questions

Several years ago, my wife and I were celebrating our anniversary on vacation in South Carolina at a wonderful resort hotel. The staff at the facility were exceptional and helped to make our stay an unforgettable experience. One evening, we had decided to venture off the property for dinner, and one of the staff offered his recommendation.

"You've got to try this place called Stewart's. Great location overlooking the water, beautiful ambiance. And it's the best seafood you'll find anywhere around."

We got into our car and set our GPS to find Stewart's. The directions indicated that we were about 15 minutes away. As we got closer to the destination, we found a lovely southern small-town scene with lots of quaint restaurants, shops, businesses, and small residences. However, after a few twists and turns, we realized we were in an area where the GPS directions weren't going to be exact. Within a mile of the restaurant, we decided to park the car, walk around, and explore the scene a bit before we got serious about finding the restaurant's exact location. We did this for about 30 minutes and had finally worked up an appetite. I called the restaurant, but interestingly enough, no one answered, and my calls kept going to voicemail.

As we stood there trying to figure out what to do, an older Southern gentleman was sitting on his porch swing watching us. I looked in his direction and smiled with a nod. He smiled back and leaned forward. With the deepest, richest Southern drawl I've ever heard, he said, "Y'all look lost."

I laughed. Nothing about this man's posture presented hostility or threat. "Yes, sir. We're looking for Stewart's."

"Oh," he replied. "Why y'all goin' there?"

"We've been told that Stewart's has the best seafood around."

"Oh, OK," he replied. "How y'all know that?"

At this point, I'd straightened up and taken another look at the man. I was born and raised on the South Side of Chicago, and several alternative responses floated in my mind. However, I remembered we were in the South, so I obliged the customs of Southern hospitality.

"They came strongly recommended," I replied quickly, adding additional bass to my voice.

The old man laughed and leaned back. "Well, I'mma tell y'all like this. If you want good seafood, trust me. Don't go to Stewart's. You'll get OK seafood. Them folks who work up at the hotels recommend Stewart's 'cause they don't live 'round here. Y'all want really good seafood? Go on down this street here one block. In the middle of the block next to the salon is Mama Sheila's Kitchen. Best seafood y'all will have in life."

My wife and I looked at each other and shrugged. Couldn't hurt. "Y'all welcome," the old man said with a wave and a smile.

When we arrived at Mama Sheila's, we found a restaurant built into an old house. It was crowded but had an intimate and cozy Southern charm that made the place warm and familiar. We were seated at the back of the house, gazing out on the water that was sparkling in the sunset. That night, my wife and I had one of the most incredible dinners we've ever had. It was amazing. Later in our stay, we finally found and tried Stewart's. The food was nowhere near as good as Mama Sheila's. The Southern gentleman was right. He was able to lead us to a better experience than the one we were planning because he was willing to challenge us with the right set of questions.

Sometimes in transition, the difference between arriving at a destination that is "just OK" and a destination that is "more than you expected" is being open to questions that challenge your direction.

Who Am I?

There's a great book called *The Purpose Driven Life* by Rick Warren. It's actually one of the best-selling books of all time next to the Bible. People became very excited about this book because, if you're like me, many of us have moments in life where we ask the questions, "What is my purpose? What am I here for?" I coach and pastor a lot of people who want to know, "What is my purpose? Why am I here? What am I here to do?" But what if one of those isn't the best first question to ask? What if the question isn't, "What should I be doing?" or "Why am I here?" What if the first question we need to ask is this: "Who am I?" What if the question of identity will give us more clarity than we think it will in helping us to navigate transition? When we deepen our awareness of our identity, that understanding will often help us to break free from the places where we become stuck in transition.

What is it about you that separates you from others? What is it about you that is unique? What are you learning about yourself in transition? What are you learning about your personality? What are you learning about your life experiences? What are you learning about who you are from your own story that's helping you know your identity? That identity will give you access to the next level and season of your life.

There's a simple, three-part question I give people to try to unpack this question of identity. It's the same as trying to find your DNA. My wife is a fan of murder mystery shows and crime investigations. In every murder investigation, one of the things they want to find is traces of DNA because if they can link the DNA found at the crime scene to a person, then they've moved closer to identifying the suspect they want to apprehend. I believe just like each of us has a unique physical DNA, we all have a unique spiritual DNA.

What about you points to the DIVINE? What is it about you inherently—about your unique expression in the world—that reminds people of God? What is it about you that just gives God glory authentically? My wife is amazing at details. I am not. I do not give God glory in detail.

My wife does. Whenever she does that, and she does it authentically, it points to the divine.

What comes NATURALLY to you? What is it you can do without putting a lot of thought or intention into it? What is it you default to doing? What are your natural abilities? What are your natural talents? What are your natural inclinations? What do you tend to drift to? Whenever you find yourself in an organization, what is the thing people consistently ask you to do? I can remember being a teenager, working in ministry, people would always ask me to help them write out their ministry plans or help them plan the strategies for what they were going to do. That's been a constant thread in my life. Throughout the course of your life, there's what we call the golden thread of preparation. There's something that's been following you your whole life that is a natural expression of the uniqueness of you.

Who are you when you're your most AUTHENTIC self? We all know what it feels like to answer the phone and clear our throat and say, "Yes, hello." But who are you when you answer the phone, and it's your best friend who's known you for 30 years? Who are you when you go into a room and you feel no pressure to put on a mask or put on a face? Who are you when you're by yourself? Think about that. That most authentic expression of you points to your identity. If you can unpack your identity, knowing who you are will give you access to the next phase of your life. Knowing who you are will help you to know what to say yes to and what to say no to.

About eight years ago, I was presented with three job offers at once. Each of those jobs was high-paying and high-profile. Each seemed like an incredible opportunity. What helped me in that situation, as I considered those amazing prospects, was a simple recognition of who I was and who God was making me become in that season. I was recognizing there were things about my unique identity I was beginning to receive.

Sometimes, God will lead you into transition so you can realize new truth about your own identity. I was realizing God was doing something divine in my preaching in that moment in my life. I was realizing God was showing me I had natural abilities I'd never used in leadership and in shepherding of people. I was realizing there were spaces when I was helping people to unpack their life journeys and understand God's Word, where I felt authentic and comfortable. My spiritual DNA wasn't directing me to any of those opportunities in that season of my life. My spiritual DNA was helping me to understand God was calling me to pastor. When I accepted that was part of my identity, along came an opportunity to be the senior pastor of a church.

You cannot be fully persuaded of your purpose without being fully persuaded of your identity. This is the problem with the way people think about vocation, and it's one of the great deceptions of our society. We live in a culture that is obsessed with production. The Industrial Age may have ended, but it has left us with an enduring belief: Anything that has true value must produce. If you don't produce something of value, then you have no value. As a result, we are all oriented to be more concerned with what we can produce than who we must become. The truth is the message of the gospel communicates to us we are *already* valuable. God gave His Son. His Son was the most valuable "thing" to Him, but He gave Him to show us just how valuable we are to Him.

We all have value. Additionally, we each have unique value. The objective, then, is not to try to produce what others value, but rather, to understand our value, and then reproduce after our own kind—express that unique value in the world.

Who I Am Tells Me What to Do

One of the jobs I was offered eight years ago was an opportunity to join the team of a very popular church as a pastor and relocate to a new city. My wife and I were living in Detroit at the time. I was excited about this opportunity for a number of reasons: a popular ministry, good pay, big city, and doing work that resonated with my values and my training. As we continued to discern and discuss the opportunity, the leadership of the church made me aware of two realities that bothered me concerning the role. "We realize this is a non-teaching role. We want you to focus on other aspects of leadership since we don't need another teacher/preacher. It's also a role where your focus will be mainly on what happens in our church, so we want someone who can make at least a ten-year commitment."

For ten years, I would need to focus locally on one church. On top of that, I couldn't teach! If I had accepted this opportunity, it would have suffocated my identity. We respectfully declined the invitation.

When we lack clarity about our identity, we embrace opportunities that interrupt our destiny. I believe sometimes Satan fights us with fiery darts, and sometimes he fights us with opportunities that look like destiny but are really distractions. The only way to know the difference is to be clear on our identity. You will experience difficulty discerning the correct next activity if you have not first discovered your most true identity. When I was able to more clearly articulate what I was learning in that season about my identity, the pastor respected my decision.

Your identity will give you direction for your transitions. Your identity will help you to know, "This next move might be just right for me." Being formed more deeply into who we are will resolve a tremendous tension going forward as we continue to ask the question, "What's next?"

CHAPTER 4
DECIDE TO SHIFT

Change is inevitable. Change for the better is a full-time job.
—Adlai E. Stevenson I

I once served a church in Detroit, Michigan. We were a new church. We didn't own a building; we were renting space for worship on Sundays, which meant that we were setting up and tearing down our worship space every week. Being a new church also meant we were very grateful when we received donations.

One day, we received a call from a ministry partner. A donor had just passed away, and the family wanted to donate the car to a church. The partner didn't have any details other than the car was in drivable condition, had a full tank of gas, and we could come pick it up when we got ready.

I caught a ride to the donor's home and met his daughter, who handed me the keys and title to the vehicle and walked me to the garage. The door opened to reveal a 1982 red Dodge Ram pickup truck. Although an older vehicle, it was kept in great condition and would prove useful to our young church.

I thanked the donor for her generosity, grabbed the title and keys, got into the truck, and tried to start the engine. It didn't start.

I tried again. No response.

Finally, the daughter came up to the car door.

"You know you have to push in the clutch, right?"

I blinked. "What's that?"

She laughed. "You don't know how to drive a stick?"

I shook my head. "I had no idea."

She graciously waited with me while my friend (who knew how to drive a stick shift) arrived to drive the truck back to the church. I would eventually learn how to drive the truck but was amazed at how different it was to drive a car with manual transmission as opposed to one with automatic. I had to be more deliberate in operating this vehicle. There were things I had to do intentionally to adjust the speed. There were levers and controls I had to pay attention to that were not in an automatic vehicle. It was humbling to be operating a vehicle that required so much more of my focus and my attention for it to function properly.

Changes Come ... Transitions Are Made

One of the most important things you can know about transition is it is not an automatic process. Transition requires thoughtful and deliberate engagement. Transition not only requires learning new skills, but it requires new ways of functioning. When you're in transition, there are realities you need to pay close attention to that you may have taken for granted in other situations. There are certain functions you can lay hold of to "shift" your life in the direction of your future. It is important you engage with these points of discernment intentionally because changes will come and go, but transitions are made.

I believe there are five key areas of discernment in transition that will help to heighten our awareness of our path, our possibilities, and our potential. The answers to these questions will not only help you to remain clear on why the transition is necessary, but they will also serve as the gears that keep you moving in the right direction.

Story

What is your story? What is the theme of your life?

Sometimes when you find yourself in transition, it's important to pay attention not just to the moment you're in, but to the theme you've learned about your life from other moments. Often, when we're in transition, particularly a painful change, we're consumed by what's happening in the moment.

It's important for us to take a step back, look at the bigger picture, and examine our larger story. A lot of the time, the answers we need for the moment that we're in are embedded in the themes of other moments we've lived through. So, we have to look back over our past and understand how God has been at work to help inform the next decision we need to make.

The Bible tells us in 1 Samuel 17 that the armies of Israel were hiding, and they were scared. They were cowering in the trenches, watching this giant named Goliath parade around and dare the armies of Israel to give him a man worthy of fighting him. David, a young boy, showed up to the battle and asked King Saul for permission to fight Goliath. Saul asked, "What makes you think that you are capable of fighting this giant?"

What was David's response? He said this:

"Well, one time I was taking care of my sheep, and a lion came after them. So, I looked at the lion, and I said, 'Where do you think you're going with my sheep?' Then I fought the lion and rescued my sheep.

"Another time, a bear came and tried to steal one of my sheep. So, I looked at the bear, and I said, 'Hey, where do you think you're going with my sheep?!' I fought the bear, and God gave me victory."

As David looked back over his story, recalled the battles he had fought and the victories he had won, he realized something: One of the consistent themes of his life was God had given him victory over things that seemed bigger and stronger than he was. By looking at the themes of his life story, David was able to understand that his experience had given him unique preparation to respond to the current problem.

Your story will give you information that might help you make sense of your current moment of transition. As you consider your life story, who have been the key characters? What have been the major conflicts? The defining moments? The conflicts that have been resolved and the lessons learned? Have the characters, circumstances, and events given you themes that seem to consistently ring true about your life? You may have experienced significant trauma. You may have suffered tremendous loss. Perhaps you have battled with issues that have caused much pain. But if you were to look at the totality of these experiences, what have they taught you about yourself? About God? About life?

Is a major theme of your life that you are wise and resourceful?

Is there a theme of your life that would suggest that you bounce back stronger after most challenges?

Are there themes that speak to your strengths? Themes that give you clues to unique abilities? Themes that help you to see more clearly why you might be facing current challenges?

Do the enemies of your present moment seem familiar in any way to past enemies? If so, how did you defeat the enemies of your past?

The themes of your story will help you make sense of the transitions you are experiencing in the present.

Heart

The second question you want to ask yourself is, *What's been on my heart?* The Bible says in Proverbs to guard your heart with all diligence, for out of it flow the issues of life. Often, when we find ourselves in transition, and we're trying to make decisions about the next move we need to make, we focus externally without doing enough work assessment and discerning of what's going on internally.

Here's a helpful acronym to help you examine the H.E.A.R.T. issues that might be influencing your transition:

What are you hurting about? Is there something that has happened, is happening, or might happen that is causing you emotional pain or distress? How is this hurt influencing the way you think, feel, and behave? Are there ways in which the hurt you are carrying might be causing you to behave that you might not be aware of? If you've ever stubbed your toe in the dark, or unexpectedly stepped on a sharp object, you know that sometimes your mouth can react to the pain in ways that can surprise you before you can determine a more appropriate response! In much the same way, our hearts often react to pain in ways that not only bypass our better judgment but also our self-awareness. One of the most subtle forces at work in transition is unprocessed hurt that undermines our discernment. The importance of having a counselor and close friends with whom you can unpack and process your hurt in transition cannot be overstated.

What are you excited about? Is there anything about the moment you are in, or the potential of your future, that excites you—that gives you hope? Is there a possibility that, when considered, literally causes you to smile? Is there anything new or pending in your life that seems to drum up extra energy or motivation? Anything that gives you fuel to keep going, even when you're tired? This is a question of passion. What are the passions of your heart telling you about the potential of your next steps? What do you wake up in the middle of the night dreaming about? Is there anything about the possibilities that are present in this moment that excite your heart in such a way that they begin to take up more space in your heart than what you may have lost in transition?

What are you anxious about? Is there something that is making you nervous? Worried? Uneasy? Is there an uncertainty that looms over you that brings with it the possibility of a less-desired outcome? Sometimes we are stuck because of negative expectations of the future that have rendered us immobile. As much as we'd like to believe that the circumstances of life beyond our control have left us stuck, sometimes we have poured cement on our own feet by our unwillingness to confront the fear of transition. If I were traveling on an airplane cruising at about 10,000 feet, standing near a large, open door, I would be considerably anxious of falling out of the airplane. A trained skydiver would not be as anxious. If both of us were on the same plane, standing by the same door, facing the same outcome, what would be the difference? The difference is that the skydiver anticipated the possible outcomes of that scenario and equipped herself for them. As you unpack and name the things that are making your heart anxious, ask yourself, "As problematic as these outcomes might be, rather than avoid them, is there a way I can be equipped to confront them?"

What are you realizing? I absolutely HATE moving. It is one of the most painstaking, draining human activities. The older I become, the more things I have to move. Our most recent move was from a home we had rented for four years to a home we purchased not far away. On moving day, as we carried boxes and furniture out of our old home, we were amazed by the things we found. Toys we thought our daughter had lost. Food particles we thought she had eaten. Money that slipped under the seat of a chair. Jewelry. Household tools that had been long replaced. Moving always pulls more energy out of us than we are willing to spend, but it also reveals more things to us that are hidden in plain sight. In the same way, the changes of life have a way of bringing realizations to us. Things we learn about life and about ourselves get exposed in times of change—things that are there but just not in plain sight. Some things are useful tools you can pick up, clean off, and use right away. Some things are waste and should have been discarded long ago. What are you realizing? What is your heart aware of now that you weren't aware of prior to the changes that unfolded in your life? What are you realizing about your personality? Your character? Your coping mechanisms? What are you realizing to be true that you didn't believe before? What do you now acknowledge as untrue that you were committed to believing before?

What are you talking about? Think beyond small talk. Transition talk is conversation that helps you discover the possibilities of your next move that your heart has picked up on before your brain. What are the topics of conversation that seem to resurface? What conversations cause you to lean forward in your seat? What issues make you ask, "Why does this keep coming up in my conversations?" What is important for you to talk about now that wasn't so important a year ago? What do you see in the world that makes your heart sing, scream, or shout in conversation? What do you find difficult to stop talking about? Pay careful attention to your transition talk. These clues might give you clarity about the invitation being extended to you as you move through transition.

Invitations

It was the summer of 2003. I had just completed my master's degree, and I had been offered a job where I was only required to work 25 hours a week, making a full-time salary with my summers off. The salary was more money than I'd ever seen in my entire life. Life was grand.

One morning, I was driving to work while the radio blasted my favorite music. I suddenly heard the voice of the Lord. Now, before you grow concerned for my mental health, God doesn't speak to me in an audible voice. The way I most often recognize God speaking to me is through an interruption in my normal train of thought that brings peace, clarity, correction, or wisdom, couched in His love.

The first thing I heard the voice say was, "Turn your radio down." So, I did.

The second thing I heard that voice say was, "You're moving to Detroit."

My first response was, "Satan, the Lord rebukes you!"

Once again, I heard the voice speak: "It's Me, Shaun. So, when you finish binding Satan, get ready to move. I'm calling you to Detroit."

A mentor of mine was starting a church in the Detroit area, and he had previously let me know he was planting this church and gathering a team of people to help it launch. When he first told me, I said, "Oh, man, that's awesome. Good for you. You go and do that." I never imagined God would call me to be part of that work. I didn't know anyone in Detroit. I didn't have any family there. I'd never started a church before. Except for college, I had never lived outside of my hometown for an extended period of time. Immediately, my mind was flooded with questions. *What did this all mean? This can't be God. How am I going to survive this? I don't have a job there. I have a job here. This doesn't make any sense. This is scary.* Yet, I had heard a clear prompting.

God had extended an invitation. There was an opportunity in front of me in that season to do, go, and be something new.

I called the manager at what I thought would be my dream job. "I've made a decision," I explained. "I'm taking a risk. I can't stay here. I've been extended an invitation to join a new project in another state."

An awkward pause followed, the silence on the other end saying everything I was already thinking. Finally, I heard a half-hearted, "Congratulations!" They released me from the job, and I helped plant that church in Detroit. It turned out to be one of the best decisions I've ever made. Not only did that decision completely alter the trajectory of my career and ministry, but I also formed deep and meaningful relationships with lifelong friends and mentors. I learned and grew in ways I could never have imagined—all because I accepted the invitation.

Invitations are the opportunities that come to you out of God's sovereignty. They are not doors that open because you kicked them down or pried them open. Often, we waste so much time trying to force pathways to open that seem right to us that we miss the invitations extended by God to go to places we've only imagined.

What are you being invited to do in this moment of your life? What pathways are opening for you? Are you being invited to give leadership in certain areas? Are you being invited to solve a continual set of problems? Are you being invited to confront a particular problem in your community? What are the options before you? We often get stuck because we can neither return to the life we know, nor can we force the path we prefer. When this happens, we can easily miss the options before us.

This is the phase of transition in which you shift your concentration away from your past and onto your possibilities. Take stock of the situation. What options are in front of you? Which invitations are consistent with the themes of your story? Which invitations give you the opportunity to respond to the issue of your heart in this season?

Feasibility

The fourth question you want to ask yourself is a very simple and practical question. *What's feasible?* What's feasible for me to do right here, where I am? What resources do I have to respond to these invitations? What's most practical?

Let's say the matter of your heart has been world hunger. You are passionate about solving the problem of people who are hungry and cannot afford their next meal. Is your next move going to be curing world hunger? Unless you can run by the ATM and grab $330 billion, probably not. From a practical standpoint, that move simply isn't feasible. Does that mean you remain stuck? No. It means you step back and ask three questions:

What is happening in my PROXIMITY? You may not have a jet that can carry you around the world and provide you with a comprehensive survey of the hunger needs. But can you find those who are hungry in your neighborhood in the next few days? You can discern the need within your immediate physical space, within your proximity, and start there. You can ask, "Who are the people and the organizations near me that can help me make this move?"

What do I have within my POSSESSION? Still haven't found that $330 billion in change between the cushions of your couch? No problem. Can you take the $5 in your pocket and go to the fast-food restaurant and get four or five sandwiches? Could you buy a few items and make a pot of soup? We grow easily disheartened by focusing on what we need to finish while underestimating the momentum that comes from focusing instead on what we need to start.

How can I respond within my POWER? You can't issue any executive orders for the military to start handing out food reserves. But you can take the resources you have and decide to share those $5 meals with five families in your neighborhood. There would be very few hurdles for you to overcome in making that simple, practical move. There probably wouldn't need to be a vote. You wouldn't have to get Congress to pass special legislation. The Board of Hunger wouldn't need to endorse you. It would be well within your ability to take action in a timeframe of your choosing.

You can apply these three questions to almost any transition decision. As you evaluate the invitations that are before you, what are the simple, practical, and proximate actions you can take with the resources that are available to you? Sometimes, we fail to do what's practical because we are distracted by what's possible. We're so focused on the finish line we can't see the starting mark. If we're going to have any kind of forward movement, if we're going to take action in times of transition, we have to begin with what's feasible and allow the things we can do that are feasible to build momentum in the direction of our future.

Tactics

The final question is one of action: *What are the key tactics involved in my next move?* What do I simply need to do? Everyone comes to a point in transition where they have to begin to ask themselves, *All right, of all the themes I see playing out in my life right now, of all the things that are on my heart, of all the things that I have been invited to do, and of all the things that are feasible for me, what am I going to do now?*

Tactics are a specific and measurable series of actions that move you from "here" to "there." Tactics work the same way as driving directions. You can make the decision you will have Chicago-style pizza for dinner, but until you map out the directions that take you from your house to the restaurant, that decision will not become reality. In other words, making the decision to transition is just the beginning of your next move.

You can answer the first four questions outlined in this section and experience the deceptive sense of peace that comes from having made a decision. After a moment of grief, loss, confusion, anger, and frustration, the fog finally clears. Your story begins to make sense. You discover there may be a greater purpose for the pain you've experienced. Hope returns. You tell your friends, your mentor, and your therapist. You spend the next several years stuck only talking about your next move.

In his book, *The Principle of the Path*, Andy Stanley perfectly states the principle we learn at this point of transition: "Direction, not intention, determines destination." When you graduate from intention to action, you will begin to experience the forward movement that can follow a transition decision.

Are you able to map out where you are and where you want to be into practical, measurable tasks you can implement in a specific space of time? Can you break down the big vision you have into practical actions?

You may want to create a business. But what is the first task in creating a business? Is it sitting down and defining your product? Is it sitting down and figuring out who your audience is? Is it developing a prototype of the product you want to serve? I know God's called you to start a church—and that might seem like a really big task—but what is the first task in doing that? Is it actually writing out the vision that God's given you for that ministry? Is it sitting down with two or three people that you know who have the same passion and fire to build a church like that with you? Is it then trying to figure out where the community is that needs that church the most?

Those simple tasks will give you clarity about what you can do, right where you are, with what you have. As you begin to do what you can, where you are, with what you have, God will do what He can (anything) where He is (everywhere) with what He has (all power)!

You Might Need to Take a Risk

The move to Detroit was a risky decision. I had very few resources and plenty of college debt. I had no connections. I would be working with some people I knew, but mostly, people I did not know. The decision to leave the certain comfort of my job and embrace the unknowns of helping to start a new church was a risk. Looking back 20 years later, I am so grateful I had the courage to take that risk, and I have no regrets.

There comes a point in some transitions you experience in life where, in order to make your next move, you must be willing to take a risk. What is a risk? A risk is a scary thing. A risk is an action that has an uncertain outcome. It's an outcome that can be influenced but not controlled. You don't know whether it's going to work out in your favor or work out against you. You don't know if it's going to move you forward or set you back. You don't know if it's going to bring you tremendous reward or tremendous regret. That's what makes a risk a risk. Sometimes, though, the shortest distance from where you are, to where you need to be, is a risk.

In 2 Kings, we see four lepers sitting outside the gates of a city. Leprosy was a highly contagious and deadly disease. If you were afflicted with leprosy, it caused a major disruption to your life. You were forced, sometimes by law, to abandon everything and everyone familiar. It often meant you could no longer keep your job. It meant you could no longer be with your family or live in your community. You were forced to quarantine. There was also no cure, so if you were quarantined, you were often living a hopeless scenario. These four lepers, having experienced a change none of them wanted, were essentially sitting and waiting for death.

But as they were sitting, something occurred to them.

> *Now there were four men with leprosy sitting at the entrance of the city gates. "Why should we sit here waiting to die?" they asked each other. "We will starve if we stay here, but with the famine in the city, we will starve if we go back there. So, we might as well go out and surrender to the Aramean army. If they let us live, so much the better. But if they kill us, we would have died anyway."*
> —2 Kings 7:3-4 (NLT)

The lepers acknowledged that the Aramean soldiers who had oppressed the region might kill them when they entered the camp. They also acknowledged they might not. They therefore deemed this decision most favorable among their available options. We learn from the story that because God was at work in the wider narrative in ways they did not know, not only did their decision pay off for them, but their risk would also play a role in ending the famine and altering the trajectory of their nation.

This is a great example of a *calculated risk*. A calculated risk is a decision made after you have examined, to the best of your ability, the possible outcomes of that decision. The risk is in choosing the most favorable outcome possible while recognizing the outcome is not at all certain. You're ready to take that risk when you have peace with the fact you cannot resolve the outcome without action. As stated before, one of the things transition teaches us is we can't control every outcome. We can plan our life, but we can't expect life to respect our plans. We don't know how any of this is going to turn out, but we do have the ability to make decisions and take actions that move us forward, not only into potentially favorable scenarios, but also into futures greater than we can ask or imagine.

Transition will bring you to a place where you can no longer sit and wait for something "right" to happen. Where the circumstances of your life have changed, and your future demands of you a response. Often, your best response will be to take a risk.

What is the risky thing you can do right now? What is the thing that, if you did it, could mean forward movement or could create a mess? What is the thing that you could do that is simultaneously daring and dangerous? What next step could you take that could reveal a path that is exciting but also anxiety-provoking?

Is it going back to school?

Is it applying for a small business loan?

Is it answering the call of God on your life and preaching your first sermon?

Is it being willing to explore a new career path?

Many people remain stuck in familiar situations because they're not willing to take the next risk. I believe God loves us too much to let us stay where we are and miss out on the rewards that come from taking certain risks. I actually believe that, in transition, God allows some pain to come as a prompt that pushes you to action.

You Might Need to Push Through Pain

One of the greatest transitions of my adult life was when my daughter was born. I was in my first pastorate and had joked with my church about possibly needing to rush out of service on Easter Sunday and leave someone else to finish the sermon if my wife went into labor. Well, not ten minutes after getting home on Easter Sunday, my wife's water broke.

In movies and television, I had always seen people rush to the hospital when the water broke. I started reacting the same way I'd seen all of the goofy husbands react. "Honey, let me get the blankets and the bags together. Don't forget to breathe!"

When we arrived at the hospital, there wasn't a hasty mob of nurses and technicians rushing my wife into an operating room. It was just a polite young woman who offered her congratulations and checked us into a large room with a single bed. Friends and loved ones came to offer prayers and well-wishes as my wife sat through hours of labor. We sat there in that room together, calm, happy, and expectant because we knew soon we would meet our daughter. The nurses and technicians came by every now and then to check on my wife and make sure she was comfortable. It was a surprisingly light and relaxed environment.

However, there eventually came a moment in which my wife started breathing heavier, and the contractions grew closer to one another. At that point, the nurses were coming into the room more frequently.

Finally, my wife's obstetrician entered the room, looked around, and clapped her hands.

"OK," she declared. "We're in the transition phase now. The energy in the room is about to shift."

Almost immediately, a hasty team of nurses and technicians entered the room with new equipment. The doctor asked my wife to identify the people who would be able to remain in the room, and everyone else had to leave. The doctor then gave everyone remaining in the room a specific assignment to help my wife prepare for labor. The energy in the room had indeed shifted!

The pains my wife experienced became more frequent and intense. At that point, she could no longer rest. She could consume no more pain medications. She could not recline. In order to help our baby come forth, my wife had to assume a position of delivery, be intentional in her breathing, and push against the pain.

Those doctors and nurses worked with my wife to time her pushes, to make sure that she was pushing at the best moment, breathing at the best moment, and resting at the best moment. I was on one side and her mom was on another side to help her maintain her position. My mother was praying and encouraging. My wife had a team to help her press through the transition phase until she delivered.

It is important to anticipate moments in transition in which your soul attempts to resist action in moments of pain. When the pain comes, the inclination will be to take a step back, pause, and try to get more comfortable. But there comes a point in every transition where you cannot remain comfortable, where you recognize comfort zones are the burial grounds of growth, and where you come to the turning point of transition. When the pain of transition intensifies, it is time to push.

You Might Need to Dream Again

About 100 years ago, a young artist from the Northwest Side of Chicago got the break of a lifetime. His brother arranged for him to get a job with an art studio in Kansas City. It was an opportunity for him to grow toward his goal of becoming a newspaper artist. After a year, he was fired for a lack of "original ideas."

He and one of his co-workers started an art company together, but it failed to attract any customers and went bankrupt after just one month. He got another job creating short films, and in his spare time, began work on another company, which also eventually went bankrupt.

After two terminations and two bankruptcies, the young man decided to try yet again. He packed his bags, moved to California, and reconnected with his brother who had just overcome a near-death battle with tuberculosis. Together, they created a character called Oswald the Lucky Rabbit, and they got a big break from a producer from New York who ordered a series based upon the character.

Things seemed to be going well until five years later, when he discovered that the producer had stolen the rights to the Oswald character right out from under him and had also hired away most of his creative team. Having been muscled out of his deal, the disillusioned young man stared blankly out of a window while on a train back to Hollywood. Disaster seemed right around the corner for his family and his company, but an idea was forming in his restless mind. He dug around for his notepad and fervently sketched his new idea on paper: a character who would later be known as Mickey Mouse. Mickey was an instant hit, and the man we know as Walt Disney began to transform the cartoon industry with huge success.

When asked about his incredible story of struggle, Walt had this to say: "All of my obstacles have strengthened me. You may not realize it when it happens, but a kick in the teeth may be the best thing in the world for you."

Despite a series of discouraging changes beyond his control, Walt decided to dream again. One of the challenges of transition is there will be moments when change happens, and we feel robbed of the life we were living. We feel as if we have been evicted from our preferred reality. In these moments, the feeling that life has forced us to accept these changes and move on as if nothing has happened can be challenging or demoralizing.

In these moments, it is vital we develop the emotional resilience to dream a new dream. Our mind can become so consumed with the comfort we lost that it can be difficult to create something new that we love. In fact, it may seem impossible. Walt Disney's story is an affirmation that sometimes the creativity that shapes our destiny is formed through our adversity.

CHAPTER 5
DECIDE TO TRUST

Life is what happens to you when you're busy making other plans.
—John Lennon

My daughter, Sage, and I have a morning routine. I usually take her to day care before starting my workday. Once we're in the car, the first thing we do is pray.

"Are you ready to pray, Little Girl?"

"Yes."

After a few minutes thanking God for His protection, peace, and blessings over our family and our day, I'll hand Sage a morning snack—usually applesauce, granola, or a banana.

Next, we'll sing songs, which Sage sometimes likes to remix.

"What would you like to sing, Little Girl?"

"Five Little Monkeys."

"OK. Five little monkeys jumping on the bed ..."

"Daddy?"

"Yes, Little Girl?"

"Sing 'Five little monkeys jumping on the car seat.'"

"You're the boss! Five little monkeys jumping on the car seat. One fell off and bumped her head …"

After about two or three songs sung two or three times, we arrive at the day care, and I drop Sage off with a hug and kiss.

One morning after beginning our routine, we prayed, and after prayer, I realized I had forgotten to grab a morning snack for Sage.

"What would you like to sing, Little Girl?"

"Daddy!" Sage exclaimed.

"Yes, Little Girl?"

"I need snack."

"Daddy forgot your snack, Little Girl. I'm sorry."

"Daddy!"

"Yes, Sage?"

"I need snack."

Clearly, she was not planning to be flexible today.

"OK. Daddy will grab a snack for you."

"Daddy?"

"Yes, Little Girl?"

"I need snack."

"I know, Little Girl. Daddy is going to get a snack for you."

"Daddy?"

"You want a snack?"

"Yes."

"Ok. Daddy knows. Please be patient, OK?"

"OK."

Thirty seconds later, "Daddy! I need snack."

As Sage continued to verify her impatience, I thought for a moment. I decided to stop at the coffee shop and order a banana via the drive-thru. There were a few cars in line, and I was nervous about the wait time, but finally, Sage stopped reminding me. *Look at that. My little girl is being patient,* I thought to myself.

We pulled out of the drive-thru, and I pulled over to prepare the banana for her to eat in her car seat. "OK, Little Girl, Daddy has a snack for you."

"No, thank you. I fine," she replied.

At first I thought, *Well, maybe it took so long that she's over it now.* Then, I realized we didn't have much time to get her to day care, so I resumed our drive. Sage had been unusually quiet for the last 10 minutes of the drive, and I thought perhaps it was because the hunger had returned. At this exact moment, right before I got out to remove her from her car seat, Sage said, "Daddy, clean mouth."

"Huh?"

"Daddy need clean mouth."

I looked in the rearview mirror and understood (with horror) what had happened. Upon getting out of the car and coming to the backseat, I realized that Sage had thrown up.

A lot.

Trying to process what happened, I noticed an empty container of applesauce sitting between her legs, immersed in the vomit.

"Sage," I said, perplexed. "Where did you get that applesauce?"

"The seat!" she exclaimed.

Then it all sank in. Sage recovered an old container of hand-held applesauce and ate the remainder of the applesauce while waiting for a snack, and this old applesauce had upset her stomach.

I learned three parenting lessons that morning:

I need to develop Sage's patience.

I need to clean out Sage's car seat every day.

Sometimes, children don't listen.

After letting the day care know about the situation and cleaning up as much of the mess as I could, Sage and I began to make our way back home. After calling the office to let them know I'd be working from home, my mother called.

"Good morning, Son. How are you?"

"Ugh ..."

I proceeded to tell my mother what had happened. "Why couldn't she have waited? Why didn't she just trust Daddy was going to meet her needs? Why don't I keep a change of clothes in the car?" I paused from my murmuring for a moment to realize my mother was laughing.

"You're laughing? Woman, have you no compassion? Your granddaughter just threw up a lake in my car, and now I'm going to miss a meeting at work. This isn't funny!"

"No, no," she explained. "I'm laughing because I prayed one day you would experience what you put me through as a toddler, so you would understand!"

"I need you to start praying differently."

The lesson I hope my daughter will eventually learn is that the outcome is always better when she chooses to trust me and wait. As I had this thought, my mother's prayer finally sank in. I realized she wanted me to understand what it felt like to want your child to trust you because as a parent, you truly know what is best. Sometimes, transition makes us hesitant. We become so afraid of the possible outcomes and unknowns of our decisions that we become tentative, fearful, and indecisive. It is in those moments that deciding to risk it is a more relevant matter to discern. However, there are also times in which transition makes us anxious. We begin to worry that if we don't make a decision, take action, and do something, bad things will happen.

Other times, we simply underestimate the weight and impact of our decision-making. We assume certain decisions can be made simply, when in reality, they should be made more soberly, patiently, and circumspectly. Every person I have ever counseled in rebuilding their lives following the transition of a divorce has said the issues ultimately causing the divorce were the result of things they had noticed prior to the marriage. I can honestly admit there are several decisions I have made in transition that I regret. Many times, I wish I had just been more patient, I had leaned on wisdom rather than intuition, or I had paid more attention to prompting than feelings. Other times, I wish I had simply trusted the Lord. Many times, I wished that instead of doing what made sense to me and attempting to do what I had believed to be God's will my way and in my time, that I had actually taken the time to wait and inquire of the Lord.

When I (Sort of) Asked the Lord ...

I once pastored an amazing congregation in the southwest suburbs of Chicago. The call to serve this church came in a most unusual way—as most of my vocational shifts have come. It was the last thing I wanted to do. Some preachers feel the need to be the lead pastor of a church, but I have never felt that need. I was perfectly content to support other pastors and occasionally preach. However, a nine-month process of discernment led me to answer the call to serve this church.

After accepting the call, I soon realized I thoroughly enjoyed serving in this role, despite dealing with difficult challenges and difficult people (myself included). At the end of year three, I had concluded I would likely be serving this congregation for some time into the future. We prayed together about a longer-term vision for my leadership in the church, which included exploring the acquisition of some adjacent property to expand our ministry campus and programs. After several months of due diligence speaking with architects, contractors, lenders, and key leaders, our church affirmed the new vision, and we officially began the process of acquiring the land.

Exactly one month later, I attended a training event with other pastors and leaders serving our denomination. During the event, I presented a workshop on healthy church culture. Immediately after the workshop, a respected denomination leader cornered me in the hallway.

"Shaun, the hand of the Lord is upon you."

"Well, glory to God. Thank you!" I responded.

"And," he continued, "I think God is calling you to a new role in leading our denomination."

"No, I don't think He is, actually," I replied, surprised by the speed with which I challenged this man's supposed prophetic utterance. "I'm quite content in my current role, and we're truly just getting started."

"I want to encourage you to pray about it."

Not wanting to hurt his feelings again, I acquiesced, "I will do that. Thank you!"

I immediately called my wife, laughing. "The folk who work in leadership of this denomination are all crazy! This guy just gave me some 'prophetic word' about me considering a national leadership role. They are insane if they think I'm leaving my church; we're just getting started!"

My wife sat and paused. After a moment, she finally asked, "Have you prayed about this?"

Whose side are you on, Woman?!

"No, I don't think I need to pray."

"That's the same thing you said about your call to pastor this church."

As soon as she said those words, my shoulders fell.

I needed to pray about this.

As we prayed about the opportunity and had further conversation, it became clear to me God had been at work, preparing me for this new assignment. It was letting go of my current assignment that God was calling me to do, despite sensible timelines, the advice of trusted mentors, and even the desires of friends and family who enjoyed having me as their shepherd.

I sat on this decision for about six months. During this time, more voices in our denomination affirmed the call to the role. Also during this time, our daughter, Sage Olivia, was born. The Sunday after my daughter's birth, I was seated in my office at the church before the morning worship service. In a few days, I would be taking paternity leave to be home with my wife and daughter as we adjusted to our new lives together.

As I sat alone in my office, I prayed.

*Lord, I have only pastored this church for four years. I just laid out a huge vision for our future together that we all believed came from You. However, the sense of call to this new role seems to be growing day by day. It doesn't make sense to me, God, but I embraced this assignment because I believed it to be Your call, and I will release this assignment if that is Your call as well. I would just ask that You speak clearly to me. Please speak clearly to me, and **I will obey You.***

A few moments later, a precious child in our church, about seven years old, knocked on my office door. She had just left her Sunday school class and held a folded piece of paper in her hand.

"This is for you, Pastor," she said. I accepted the paper, and she walked away.

I closed the door and sat back down at my desk. I unfolded the paper and read these words:

God wants you to obey Him.

I sank into my chair and wept. *This was God being as clear as clear gets.*

At that moment, I recalled more wise words from my grandmother:

"Never ask God a question unless you're ready for the answer."

Even though this prompting was clear, it was not the answer that I wanted. So, I resisted this message for another several months. And during my time of resistance, I became like Jonah, and God rocked my boat. I finally said yes to the new role and made the decision to leave my beloved congregation.

Though this transition decision was a difficult one, and letting go was not easy, there were a series of affirmations that would follow over the next two years that I had made the right decision. There were connections I would make that I could not see. There were assignments I would be in position to complete. There were resources to be shared. There were leaders to encourage, partnerships to be formed, and defining moments to be experienced that would nourish and transform my soul.

Had I made my decision based upon what made sense to me at the time, I would have missed the invitation God was extending for me to experience something beyond my understanding. Asking the Lord for wisdom beyond my natural ability helped me to make a decision that, once again, altered the trajectory of my life.

Because God is omniscient (knows all things) and omnipresent (is in every place at every time), He has insight into our life and the possibilities of our path that we could never gather through natural means. There is peace that comes from making the choice to trust what He knows. In spite of the fact that we have free will, God sees more than we do, knows more than we do, and loves us, and His direction can be trusted.

But They Did Not Ask the Lord …

In Joshua 9, the children of Israel, now under Joshua's leadership, had already crossed the river Jordan, had already marched around the walls of Jericho, and had already begun to divvy up the Promised Land by tribe. Now, they were recovering from a terrible experience at Ai. Ai is notable for being the scene of a humiliating Israelite defeat as the small city of Ai routed the Israelites and inflicted three dozen casualties. The loss at Ai was due to the sin of Achan (Joshua 7:1-5). In direct defiance of God's command to keep nothing for themselves from the wicked city of Jericho (Joshua 6:19), Achan had kept a robe, two hundred shekels of silver, and a fifty-shekel bar of gold and hid it all in a hole he had dug within his tent. Achan kept his theft a secret until Israel was defeated at Ai. God then revealed to Joshua the cause for this defeat, and Achan, his family, and everything he owned was destroyed at God's command (Joshua 7:25-26).

Once Israel had purged sin from the camp, God finally granted them a decisive victory over Ai, and the fame of Israel's God spread throughout the land. This victory made the other inhabitants of Canaan nervous. Israel was commanded by God to drive out all the inhabitants of the land. It is then that the other nations realized, "Uh-oh! We're next!"

Most of these nations devised a strategy to try working together to defend themselves against Israel in head-on combat. However, the Gibeonite nation had a different plan.

> But when the people of Gibeon heard what Joshua had done to Jericho and Ai, they resorted to deception to save themselves. They sent ambassadors to Joshua, loading their donkeys with weathered saddlebags and old, patched wineskins. They put on worn-out, patched sandals and ragged clothes. And the bread they took with

them was dry and moldy. When they arrived at the camp of Israel at Gilgal, they told Joshua and the men of Israel, "We have come from a distant land to ask you to make a peace treaty with us."

The Israelites replied to these Hivites, "How do we know you don't live nearby? For if you do, we cannot make a treaty with you."

They replied, "We are your servants."

"But who are you?" Joshua demanded. "Where do you come from?"

They answered, "Your servants have come from a very distant country. We have heard of the might of the Lord *your God and of all he did in Egypt. We have also heard what he did to the two Amorite kings east of the Jordan River—King Sihon of Heshbon and King Og of Bashan (who lived in Ashtaroth). So, our elders and all our people instructed us, 'Take supplies for a long journey. Go meet with the people of Israel and tell them, "We are your servants; please make a treaty with us."' This bread was hot from the ovens when we left our homes. But now, as you can see, it is dry and moldy. These wineskins were new when we filled them, but now they are old and split open. And our clothing and sandals are worn out from our very long journey."*

So the Israelites examined their food, but they did not consult the Lord.
—Joshua 9:3-14 (NLT)

The Gibeonites realized they did not have the means to defeat Israel, so they would need to figure out a way to remain on their land. They ultimately came up with a plan to disguise themselves as travelers from a faraway land who were weary and fatigued from their long journey. If the Israelites were compassionate upon them, then they would be able to make a treaty which would allow them to remain on the land and keep them safe from the threat of war.

Their plan would not have worked had it not been able to exploit one major mistake made by the people of Israel: They did not inquire of the Lord.

They were deceived by what they HEARD: "We are strangers from a faraway land. We're not your enemies. We want peace with you."

They were deceived by what they SAW: They examined their fake provisions.

They were deceived by what they FELT: They concluded, based upon a vague story and deceptive evidence, that these "foreigners" could be trusted.

Because they did not inquire of the Lord, they were deceived, and they deceived themselves. The Lord knew things they did not know and understood things that they could not see. As a result of their decision-making, the Israelites were now sworn to keep peace and share their property with an enemy.

What is playing the role of a Gibeonite in your life? What do you need to remove from your life that has deceived you into allowing it to overstay its welcome? What is trying to trick you away from trusting God in transition?

Is it a relationship you know is not healthy, yet you have an emotional or historical attachment?

Is it an opportunity that SEEMS RIGHT but doesn't really allow you to be YOU?

Is it a secret, stubborn habit that lies to you and tells you that it won't do you any real harm? After all, everyone's got SOME issue, right?

The Gibeonites in your life might present you with a way forward that seems right, but the real question is this: Have you inquired of the Lord? Sadly, many people wait until they find themselves in crisis before they consider praying. They fail to realize God knows what they do not know and delights in giving them wisdom, guidance, direction, and counsel about their decisions before they ever find themselves in danger.

Have you stopped to figure out if God has anything to say about the turning point you've found yourself in? Have we worked to desensitize ourselves from our fallen ego? Have we deepened our awareness of truths that don't always sit in plain sight? Have you considered the influence of your ego? Your anxiety? Your selfish ambition? Your pride? Have you assessed whether or not your fears are making you believe you MUST make a decision RIGHT NOW when in reality, none may be required at the moment?

We invite all sorts of problems in transition when we fail to trust God.

We Invite Delays

My consulting work often requires me to travel, sometimes to familiar places, and sometimes to places I've never been. One particular trip led me to Central Indiana, not far from Marion, Indiana, and my alma mater, Indiana Wesleyan University. While in college, I had driven that route from Chicago to Marion so many times that I knew it like the back of my hand. I had learned all of the shortcuts, the best rest stops, and the roads to avoid at peak travel times. However, this particular trip would be the first time I had driven that route in over 15 years. When I got on the road, I started off without a GPS, trying to see how much of the route I would remember. Slowly, it started coming back to me. I was excited to see familiar landmarks and rest stops. I remembered specific stretches of road where I had prayed and the music I had listened to (then on my cassette player) as I drove.

After some time, the route became unfamiliar. At that point, I decided to turn on my GPS to make sure that I was still moving in the right direction. As soon as I set the direction, my GPS spoke: "Continue on this road for 90 miles."

90 miles? That can't be right, I thought. I had already been on that road for about an hour; another 90 miles would have me passing the exit I used to take. I calculated alternate routes and reset the GPS.

"Continue on this road for 80 miles."

This thing must not know Indiana.

After about 30 more miles, I noticed a familiar exit and decided that I would take that exit and continue on the road I knew. My GPS immediately rebuked me.

"When possible, make a legal U-turn."

Not necessary. I know where I am now!

I continued on the road I knew, driving through a small town that hadn't changed much in 15 years. About two hours later, I did arrive in Marion, but about 40 minutes later than the arrival time my GPS had previously calculated. Apparently, the roads had changed significantly since my college days, which had created a much faster route between Chicago and Marion. Fortunately, I enjoyed reminiscing while taking the scenic route—which had once been a shortcut. In God's mercy, I made it to my destination, but not as quickly as I could have.

How much time do we waste traveling the road that seems right to us? How much delay, distraction, and unnecessary waste of resources do we cause our lives when we take turns and exits that make sense to us but go against the seemingly strange direction of the Lord?

We Invite Disappointment

There is a sober warning given in the words of Psalm 95.

> *Listen to God's voice today! Don't be stubborn and rebel as your ancestors did at Meribah and Massah out in the desert. For forty years they tested God and saw the things he did. Then God got tired of them and said, "You never show good sense, and you don't understand what I want you to do." In his anger, God told them, "You people will never enter my place of rest."*
> —Psalm 95:7-11 (CEV)

This warning references an event that is recorded in Numbers 20. The children of Israel were continuing their journey toward the Promised Land of Canaan. This would be a 40-year journey that should have taken less than three weeks. Why was their journey so long? The Israelites could not trust God.

They could not trust God's power because they were afraid to fight with the inhabitants of the land that lived along the faster route, so God led them on a slower route. He knew if they had to fight, they might become afraid and return to Egypt (Exodus 13:17).

They could not trust God's provision because they complained there wasn't enough food. Even though God blessed them with manna from heaven, they complained about not having meat, cucumbers, melons, onions, and garlic which they had enjoyed while they were slaves in Egypt (Numbers 11).

They could not trust God's protection. When the spies surveyed the land, the majority opinion was discouraging. "The land we explored devours those who inhabit it. All of the people we saw were very large. We were like grasshoppers in their eyes!" (Numbers 13) After this, the nation of Israel complained against Moses and murmured among themselves before God. The Lord had heard enough.

> "How long must I put up with this wicked community that keeps complaining about me? ... Your bodies will drop dead in this desert. All of you who are at least 20 years old, who were registered and listed, and who complained about me will die."
> —Numbers 14:27-29 (GW)

By Numbers 20, the surviving generations had started to complain again. This time, there was no water for them to drink, and their anxiety caused them to harden their hearts against God just like their ancestors had.

Moses is given a clear directive from God:

> "Take the staff, and you and your brother Aaron gather the assembly together. Speak to that rock before their eyes and it will pour out its water. You will bring water out of the rock for the community so they and their livestock can drink."
> —Numbers 20:8 (NIV)

Though Moses had been faithful and resilient in his leadership of the untrusting people of Israel, his frustration had reached a peak.

> So Moses took the staff from the Lord's presence, just as He commanded him. He and Aaron gathered the assembly together in front of the rock and Moses said to them, "Listen, you rebels, must we bring you water out of this rock?" Then Moses raised his arm and struck the rock twice with his staff. Water gushed out, and the community and their livestock drank.

> But the Lord said to Moses and Aaron, "Because you did not trust in Me enough to honor Me as holy in the sight of the Israelites, you will not bring this community into the land I give them." These were the waters of Meribah, where the Israelites quarreled with the Lord and where He was proved holy among them.
> —Numbers 20:9-13 (NIV)

God wanted Moses to trust Him enough to speak to the rock and cause water to come forth. This would have been a demonstrative reminder of God's power to the children of Israel. However, Moses did not trust God, and his decision to disregard God's instruction would ultimately cause him to be kept out of the Promised Land.

Can you imagine hearing God say this? After years of great leadership and victory, years of waiting and hoping for the Promised Land, decades watching people you love die in the wilderness, survived only by their youngest children, year after year of enduring complaints, attacks, and your own insecurities ... only to realize it would all come to disappointment because you had one minute of mistrust in God's direction.

How many times have we experienced disappointment in transition because we allowed our fears and our frustration to drive our actions? How many times have we done what made sense and caused ourselves to miss out on a miracle? How many times have we failed to trust because we were more confident in what we could do in our own strength and ability?

In transition, when we allow our feelings to undermine our discernment, we either begin to over-function, or we grow hesitant about trusting the Lord's voice, we harden our hearts, and we invite disappointment.

We Invite Destruction

First Chronicles 14 explains that Saul, King David's predecessor, died because he was unfaithful to the Lord. After a victorious battle, Saul was supposed to wait for Samuel to come and offer a sacrifice. However, Saul grew impatient. He thought the sacrifice couldn't wait for Samuel's arrival, so he took it upon himself to offer the sacrifice, which went against the law of the Lord.

The Lord instructed Saul to kill every living thing in battle. However, Saul spared some animals that he thought were good enough to keep. Samuel rebuked Saul, telling him that "obedience is better than sacrifice."

Later, after Samuel died, King Saul was desperate for the counsel that the faithful judge, priest, and prophet had once provided. Instead of going to God, Saul sought a medium, the witch of Endor, for guidance because he thought it would be best if someone conjured the spirit of Samuel to speak with him.

Sometimes, we fail to inquire of the Lord because we think we already know what God is saying. As I consider my own life, it is amazing how many times I have confused my thoughts, my feelings, and my inclinations with God's voice. And it is mortifying to realize how often I consulted with strange or shady sources for direction and counsel rather than prayer or wise counsel.

It was Saul's overconfidence in his own thinking and the resulting decisions that caused the Lord to remove His anointing and direct Samuel to anoint a man after God's own heart, David, the son of Jesse, to be the next king. The rest of Saul's life was wrought with anger, jealousy, and strife before it finally ended in a dishonorable death and destruction for his family. When we trust any other source than God for direction and guidance, we place our lives in serious danger.

Isaiah 55:8 (NIV) says, "'My thoughts are nothing like your thoughts,' says the Lord, 'and My ways are far beyond anything you could imagine.'" Simply put, God thinks differently than we do. I remember receiving the call in early December of 2002 that my grandmother was on her way to the hospital, and it wasn't good. I remember racing to the hospital, praying all the way that the Lord would heal her and believing that she would live. Yet, she died. I had completely ignored her desire to go home and be with God, her desire that God would *heal her by ending her suffering*, that her pain would cease, that she would finally be reunited in heaven with loved ones she had missed for decades, that despite the fact that she was only 71 years old, she was ready to meet Jesus. In my unwillingness to grieve losing her, I was praying for God to prolong her life while she was praying for God to allow her life to peacefully end. The Lord honored her prayer, and she passed away a few weeks before Christmas. God and I thought differently.

On another occasion, I was asked by a family to pray for their daughter because she was dying. For some reason, I thought, *I shouldn't pray. What if God's desire is NOT to heal her?* The doctors had rendered their assessments, so I ignored a still, small voice and prayed for comfort for the family. A week later, that young girl was sitting up eating in her hospital bed. She graduated college a year later. God and I thought differently.

In each case, I wasn't nearly as interested in hearing God's thoughts or knowing God's ways as I was in making sure God would hear ME. In each case, I regretted not listening for and trusting the Lord's voice. I will say, the decisions I have regretted most have been the ones I thought I could make without consulting God—the ones that sounded and seemed and felt right to me.

SOMETIMES, God doesn't always ask us to make decisions about the direction of our lives as much as He asks us to discern and trust His direction.

That's hard when I know what I want.

That's hard when I know how I think.

That's hard when I know what I would prefer.

That's hard when I think I know what makes sense already.

Recovering from decisions we make without *seeking to know what we don't yet know* can have disastrous effects upon our lives.

The congregation of Israel did not inquire of the Lord in order to learn what it did not know. The people did what they felt to be right, not what

God was saying. They ended up affirming a deception. They did not seek God for the truth. They ended up making peace with their enemies.

However, there is a redemptive grace hidden in the story of the Gibeonite deception. The Gibeonites said, "We knew that God was going to give you favor to drive us out, so we were afraid." These people had more faith in God than the Israelites had. God used Israel's failure in discernment to allow mercy to be shown to the Gibeonites, a foreign people. This is a foreshadowing of God's grace which would be extended to the Gentiles in spite of the Israelites.

This is good news for us. It reminds us that God's grace works in our transitions in spite of our inability to get things right.

In spite of our mistakes.

In spite of our fears.

In spite of our self-deception.

In spite of our disagreement with the all-confusing ways of God.

It becomes a cautionary tale for us in transition. Our decisions will either position us to see God's grace work *through us* or *in spite of us*. Eventually, transition helps us decide to trust God and to trust the most difficult realities of change.

Trust the Unwanted

In Matthew 26, Jesus is facing an unparalleled moment of transition. He is about to be betrayed by someone in his inner circle, arrested on false charges, brutally beaten, critically wounded, wrongly convicted, publicly humiliated, and agonizingly executed. He is fully aware of the immensity of physical and emotional pain He is about to experience, and prior to the sequence of events leading to His crucifixion, He paused in the Garden of Gethsemane for a moment of prayer.

Essentially, Jesus said, "This is not what I want." He went on to say, "Father, if it be possible, let this cup (this suffering I'm about to experience) pass from me." The interesting thing about this prayer is Jesus is God, so He already knew another way wasn't really possible. He also knew how everything would turn out in the end, yet He expresses His honest desire to avoid the pain of this horrible and humiliating moment of transition.

Maybe you are facing a transition you did not want.

Perhaps you are facing a foreclosure or eviction and have exhausted all possibilities for an alternative outcome.

Perhaps you have been fired or laid off from a job recently, and you are preparing for a transition period in which you know that eventually, any resources you have saved will run out, and you are preparing for the unwanted agony of worry about how to pay your bills and provide for your family.

Maybe you are preparing to let go of a loved one in hospice care and have realized God has decided not to respond to your prayers that He would heal them in the ways you had hoped. I have many painful memories of realizing that God, in His sovereignty, had chosen not to intervene as I had hoped as I faced moments of change and loss. I know how it feels when your prayers don't "work" and to wonder ...

Did I not pray hard enough?

Does God not care about me?

Is God not as powerful as He claims to be?

Did I do something to deserve this?

Well, what is the use of praying anyway, if my prayers won't change the outcome?

In those moments, it has become comforting to know Jesus understands.

The Bible says Jesus prayed very hard, in fact, so hard that He began to perspire drops of blood. Despite His prayers, change brought Him an unwanted outcome.

Jesus was God's only divinely conceived Son. He was the only person to walk the earth with the nature of being fully human and fully God (1 Timothy 2:5-6). Jesus was God's Son "in whom I am well pleased" (Matthew 3:17). So, we know He was loved and precious to God, and Jesus had not done anything to deserve the pain that He experienced. His response? "Not My will, but Thine be done" (Matthew 26:39).

There are many situations in which I truly believe my prayers HAVE changed my circumstances. Therefore, I know prayer works, but I don't know why it doesn't work sometimes when I want my prayers to take away the situations I don't want. I believe Jesus understood that sometimes prayer doesn't just change our outcomes; it changes our hearts, so we can reconcile and accept what God has allowed.

During my first pastorate, one of my parishioners had a massive heart attack and was in ICU on life support. I prayed with the family who had chosen to affirm life and trust God's ability to heal this loving woman. I joined them in this prayer, hoping for the best outcome. Oddly enough, after our last moment of prayer, her elderly mother asked her son to take her home. "You don't want to stay and wait, Mom?"

"No," she said. Then she came over to me and said, "My daughter is leaving us tonight. Please pray with me as I go in to say goodbye."

The prayers of this wise mother had allowed her to sense what God was allowing. We wanted our prayer to change God's will, but prayer had changed hers. Eventually, we would all change our prayers and ask God to comfort us with the strength to let her go.

Not my will. But thine be done.

The example of how Jesus responded to unwanted transition helps me greatly. It helps me to know that even while sharing the nature of God and having all of the answers, Jesus understands when we want something desperately, when we have a specific request, and when we want to avoid something. Even though He knows (and we also often know) everything will work out in the end, Jesus knows sometimes we just want things to be different. He also shows us how to accept it and trust God when we realize that what we want simply isn't what God is allowing to happen. He teaches us our prayers won't always change our changes, but our prayers can change us to embrace change.

Not my will, but thine be done.

Trust the Unexpected

In the introduction to this book, one of the ways I describe change is as a "force." One way my faith compels me to think of change is it works as an agency that administers the superintendence of God in our lives. The idea of God's superintendence helps me to understand the dance between God's sovereignty and my free will. I am not a robot that decides and behaves in ways that have all been predetermined. However, my decisions and actions are subject to the whim of an all-loving, all-knowing, and all-powerful God who orchestrates the situations and circumstances of my life in ways I understand and ways I may not now (or ever) comprehend. Change agents I cannot control can either be used by God to help me make decisions, take action, or simply learn some of the most basic lessons of life:

Life is not all about me. (I am not the center of the universe.)

I may learn from the past, but I may not control the future.

My plans will change, and life will go on.

The year 2013 taught me some transforming lessons about transition and the superintendence of God. By that time, I had known my good friend and mentor, Rev. Dr. Larry Lee Sherman, for nearly 10 years. Larry was a silver-haired sage. Although he was a few inches shorter than me in height, he was a giant in ministry and a mentor and friend to me and many others. He served as a denominational leader who worked primarily to start new churches and coach pastors. For half the time I knew Larry, I was blessed to serve with him as an apprentice and an assistant coach to those new churches. Larry was a wise and effective pastor who had planted two strong, thriving churches that continued to live on long after he left them.

I often had the chance to journey with Larry to visit and consult with some of the churches he helped to start. In the many times of transition to these churches by car and by plane, Larry and I would talk about life, ministry, and all things in between. In the winter of 2012, I shared with Larry I felt a pervasive restlessness I could only interpret as a prelude to transition. Moreover, my wife and I had developed a strong sense through prayer we would experience transition and relocation sometime in the next year. There were several possible pathways for me to consider in such a transition: plant a new church, assume the pastorate at an existing church, or accept any similar job working with a church or organization. While we were open to relocating anywhere, we felt a particular sense our next transition would lead us back home to Chicago.

I unpacked as much as I could make sense of for Larry, certain that in his consistently clear and pragmatic form, he would plainly articulate God's plan for my life and tell me exactly what to do. When I finished, Larry paused a moment. After staring off down the snowy road, he adjusted his glasses to the bridge of his nose and cleared his throat. "You know," he began. "Recently, I heard one of the best sermons on transition. One of his central points was this: We don't really plan for transitions, and that's not our job anyway. Our job is not to plan but to prepare. Since God is sovereign, our responsibility is to make sure that we are most prepared for wherever the Lord may lead us."

"Wow," I said. "That's a really good word." After a moment, I asked, "So, how do you think I should prepare?"

Larry smiled, "Ya know, let me think about it."

Over the next few months, over coffee, lunch, birthday celebrations, team meetings, and church visits, Larry would pour out more wisdom and practical insights to help me think about how to prepare for where God was leading, even though we both had no idea about what exactly I was preparing for. Several opportunities emerged—none of which I felt compelled to accept. Despite that, the conversations, prayer, and discernment kept going.

In our last conversation, Larry and I talked for nearly four hours. Months earlier, Larry had said, "Let me think about it," in reference to the question of how Veronica and I should prepare. This conversation would prove to me that Larry had been thinking deeply and intentionally about his response. The wisdom he shared with me helped affirm why I appreciated him. He gave practical suggestions, at each point acknowledging the sovereignty of God and the discernment of my wife:

"Think carefully before you buy a house or put down roots in any neighborhood ... you might not settle in a role for a while ... and that's OK."

"Never make a major career decision before you and your wife have prayed, fasted, and explored your options."

"Spend and save wisely."

"Consider going back to school to pursue more training, and be intentional with professional development experiences. It adds to your expertise and to your value."

"Write."

"Take care of your health. Ministry is a marathon, not a sprint."

"Guard your integrity with your life!"

As we concluded, Larry summarized his download of wisdom. "Several paths could emerge for you, Shaun: You could pastor an existing church, you could plant a church, or you could take on a denominational leadership role. In two or three years, you could have *my* job. You have the gifts, heart, and skills to do any of these or other things well *and* be fruitful even as you grow. Just remember to prepare more than you plan, because we never know exactly how life will turn out. When things happen that you haven't anticipated, Shaun, just trust God. He will lead and guide you if you keep your heart open to what He wants to do with your life. I'm excited to see how the Lord will use you, and I will be there to support you however I can."

Even though I still had no idea what path might unfold, I left that meeting extremely encouraged about my future and so very grateful I would embrace the future knowing Larry committed to being there to provide coaching and support in his usually wise, caring, and faithful way.

Just three days later, I received a phone call from Jody, our team administrator.

"Larry Sherman passed away this morning."

After a pause, the information finally registered. My mouth responded with a litany of questions, but I wasn't listening to the answers. My mind was racing. Larry was only a few weeks away from a two-month sabbatical where he and his wife Debbie had planned to rest, travel, and spend time with their beloved grandkids.

He had prepared us for a temporary absence. Not for this.

I immediately felt deep sadness for his wife and family, for our team, for the leaders and churches we served together, and for myself.

Life does not always agree with us on which things should remain certain. I was OK with not knowing what my next step would be vocationally because I thought I knew what to expect relationally. I thought no matter what choices came my way, Larry would be there to help me think and process. If I would pastor a church, Larry would be there to install me. If I planted a church, Larry would be there to coach me. If I took on a denominational role, Larry would be there to collaborate with me.

I had embraced the idea of preparing versus planning, but this was definitely not the plan.

As our team grieved together and worked to fill the chasm left by Larry's sudden death, I was reminded of an important lesson God had taught me over and over again.

A lesson I was taught when my family became homeless.

A lesson I was taught when my cousin was gunned down at the age of 22.

A lesson I was taught when my wife and I decided to relocate to Michigan.

A lesson I was taught when I quit my job to launch my consulting company.

A lesson I was taught at every major turning point in my life.

The single most important decision to make in transition is to **TRUST GOD.**

I believe with all of my heart in the words I've written throughout this book. I believe it is important for us to make decisions. I believe it is important for us to realize when it is time to leave certain environments, situations, and circumstances. I believe it is important for us to realize the uniqueness of our own identity, and how an awareness of who we really are can help inform our choices in transition. It is important to learn how to take risks and understand the windows of opportunity that are before you to make your next move.

However, there have come times in my life where I have learned that when transitions came, and it was time to make some decisions in order to move forward, what seemed to be my only choice was the **best one:**

"Shaun, just TRUST GOD."

Trust Him in times of death, loss, and uncertainty.

Trust Him more than intuition and instincts.

Trust Him more than the counsel of friends.

Trust Him more than hopes, dreams, and expectations.

Trust Him more than formulas, strategies, or the lessons that fill the pages of books.

Right about now, I know what you're thinking. It feels like a setup, doesn't it? Have I just neared the finish of this book only to discover what I've just read may not work?

Not quite. You need to have strategies. You need to dream. You need to think. You need to prepare. You need to form relationships. You need to be intentional. But you also need to know what to do if (and when) none of that stuff works.

Trust the Unknowns

In Acts 1, Luke tells his friend Theophilus of the events that transpired in the lives of the disciples after Jesus died and was raised from the dead. We know Jesus showed Himself for 40 days "with many infallible proofs." We also know Jesus led his disciples to a hill from which He ascended into heaven. Before He left, the disciples asked Jesus a question: "Lord, at this time, will you restore the Kingdom to Israel?"

As per usual, Jesus gave the disciples a very interesting reply: "It is not for you to know times or seasons that the Father has fixed by His own authority."

Transition helps us to realize there are some things we just won't know or understand. Those things are "above our pay grade" and fixed according to the Father's sovereign authority. These things simply need to be accepted. As difficult as it may be, a key thing transition teaches us to accept is God's timing.

Notice the disciples did not ask "IF" Jesus would restore the Kingdom; they asked "WHEN." Even though they did not yet fully understand Jesus' continuing mission and plans for them, they continued to affirm their hope that Jesus would ultimately liberate the people of Israel from foreign oppression.

Like the disciples, we reach a point in our following Jesus through transition where the question is no longer, "Will God do it?" because over time we gain greater understanding of His heart, and we learn to trust the integrity of His Word. In other words, we eventually learn that if God said it, then we can trust He will do it. While we may no longer wonder, "Will He?" our question now is, "When will He?" Even when we trust the truth of His promise, we can still struggle to trust the timing of His process. The disciples were unable to receive a timetable for their hopes, dreams, and expectations. But they would soon learn, by God's grace and with the Spirit's power, they could trust God's timing.

When God fails to perform His promises within our desired timeframe, we tend to become anxious. Sometimes we begin to wonder whether or not God even cares. Our problem is a faulty perspective on the activity of God. We fail to realize God's timing is completely different from our own. Not only that, but God's abilities are not bound by our time constraints.

I once had some consulting work to finish that required graphic design, and I chose a subcontractor who lived in Bangladesh. I had a deadline, and I needed him to complete an assignment, so I could present a fully completed project to my client. I needed a design to drop into a document that I had planned to share in a meeting on a Monday at 9 a.m. Initially, my subcontractor said the soonest he could get it done was 7 a.m. on Monday. I was worried the timeframe would be too tight, but by that time I had no other choice. I stressed myself out about it all day Friday. I checked in with him numerous times on Saturday, and he said, "I'm sorry, the earliest I can do is by 6 a.m. on Monday." I hardly slept Saturday night and was a nervous wreck by Sunday afternoon. After dinner, I paced my home-office floor. What would I say to my clients if I couldn't produce this deliverable on time? I was considering all types of worst-case scenarios in my head. Finally, around midnight, I had decided I had done all I could do, and I would just go to bed, try to get some sleep, and hope for the best. Before I went to bed, I checked my email and realized earlier that evening around 7 p.m. my subcontractor had sent me the completed assignment.

"Thank you, Jesus!" I exclaimed in relief. I immediately sent him a bonus payment and said, "Thanks for getting it in to me early!"

He replied back almost instantly, saying "Hey, thanks for the bonus, but I'm not early; I'm on time." He reminded me the time zone in Bangladesh is 11 hours ahead of Chicago, and it was already several hours past 9 a.m. there. He had completed and sent me the graphic I needed five hours before I realized it.

While I was worried about whether or not he would be able to get it done when I needed it, I actually got what I needed early because he was actually on time. Had I remembered he operated in a different time zone than I, I would've had a much more restful weekend!

God operates in a completely different time zone than we do because God exists outside of time as we know it. What this means is God is not stressed by the things that stress us. We worry about certain things happening before we reach a certain age, but God has already seen us older than that age, and He knows our strength will be even greater. He is also not nearly as worried as we are about the future because God has already seen it. As long as our heart's posture is to be faithful to what we know, God will handle the future we don't know.

One of the most life changing books I've ever read was *The Will of God as a Way of Life* by Gerald Sittser. I read this book after Larry's death, when all kinds of realities I had never planned were unfolding. The book challenged the way I had learned to think about life calling and vocation.

I had always believed God had a plan for us, and the sooner we figure out His plan, the better. Once we learn God's will for our lives, we could then do God's will. For the most part, this put me in a place of constant anxiety. My typical frame of mind was, "If I miss the will of God, I'm gonna screw up my life!" This thinking made me anxious about most "big" decisions. I began to fear if I did not make "the right choice," I could run the risk of missing the will of God for my life. I feared if I didn't figure out how to perfectly plan out my path, I could be jeopardizing my future. Sittser presents a different way of thinking on our decisions:

> "We never truly know how things will turn out. What appears in our minds to be the pathway we should take might change as suddenly as weather in the Midwest. So, we would be wise to be attentive and responsive to God along the way, even in matters that appear to have little significance ... perhaps

our attention to these 'little things' is the Will of God, and
our preoccupation with the future a foolish distraction."
—Jerry Sittser, *The Will of God as a Way of Life*

This wisdom has helped me whenever I have found myself being driven by a fear of making the wrong decision. There have been many times where I felt like I had made all of the right decisions, yet my vision for the future didn't come to pass. There have also been times where I felt I had made all of the wrong decisions, and somehow, my next steps unfolded in unimaginably good ways.

I think the truth is, no matter how much we think, pray, strategize, or contemplate, there will come some transition moments where we won't have all of the information we need, times when we won't know how to plan or prepare for what may come next, or times when we won't be able to make the "big decision." We won't be able to solve for all of the variables in our formulas. There will come moments of transition where we think we're on the right road, and suddenly, the road will bend sharply or lead us to what feels like a dead end. In those moments, our best option is to *do what we know, and trust God with what we don't know.*

Sage and I didn't always have a morning routine. When she first began day care, Veronica would typically drop her off, and I would pick her up. One morning when Sage was about six months old, Veronica had to go to an early morning meeting and was unable to take her to day care, so I had the task of both getting Sage ready for day care and dropping her off, which made my wife nervous. This would be the first time I would be getting Sage ready for day care on my own. It was up to me to feed her, bathe her, dress her, and drive 30 minutes to get Sage to day care by no later than 9 a.m.

Veronica left that morning for her meeting around 6:30 a.m. I was sitting on the side of the bed, next to Sage's bassinet. Veronica looked earnestly at me to seek confirmation: "You got this, Shaun Marshall?"

"Yes, honey. We'll be fine."

Then, Veronica left.

The next thing I knew, Sage was crying. I looked up, disoriented. Somehow, I had fallen back asleep. I checked the clock: 7:30. I had one hour to prepare myself and bathe, feed, dress, and get Sage to day care before the cut-off time. Veronica had already laid out the clothes Sage was to wear for the day.

I've got this. No problem, I thought.

I thought wrong.

After bathing Sage, it was about 7:50, and I made the ultimate rookie parent-of-an-infant mistake: I dressed her and THEN gave her something to eat.

At about 8:15, Sage and I were both ready. I grabbed her diaper bag and was ready to carry her to the car. At the exact moment I looked in Sage's direction, she spit up enough fluid to fill an Olympic-sized pool. Her clothes were completely soiled, and now I had to clean her up and find new clothes for her to wear.

By the time I had Sage cleaned up and ready to go again, I checked the clock: 8:40.

This was a problem. The drive was 30 minutes, and if I didn't get Sage to day care by 9 a.m., I would need to either find a babysitter so I could go on to work or call off for the day.

After strapping Sage into her car seat and exiting the driveway, my wife called on a break. "What time did you get Sage to day care?" she asked.

After a moment of trying to decide whether or not I would lie, I confessed everything that had taken place that morning. It's important to note my wife is also a Christian, which means that she prays *before* she cusses. So, after a moment of silence, she began to pray: "Lord, please help my fool husband get our daughter to day care quickly and safely."

I raced as cautiously as I could to the day care, taking every shortcut I knew, but there were still delays. When we finally arrived at the day care, it was about 10 minutes after 9 a.m. The day care is known for having a strict policy around dropping children off on time, so while I knew Sage would be unable to attend for the day, and I would need to make other arrangements, I decided to go to the front desk to let the administrator know why Sage would be absent that day.

Sage and I entered the building, both of us looking defeated. The administrator smiled and said, "First time dropping off, Dad?"

"Yes," I said in defeat. "I know that we're too late. I just wanted to let you know that Sage and I ran into some unforeseen difficulties this morning, so she'll be back in day care tomorrow."

The administrator smiled. "Actually Mr. Marshall, you are late, but you can still go ahead and take Sage to her classroom. She is an infant, and the infant classroom has an hour grace period."

Cue the Hallelujah Chorus.

Despite the fact I had made mistakes, and despite my poor decisions, and despite the obstacles I faced during the drive, and despite the fact I was late, Sage and I were still able to get where we needed to go, all because there was grace waiting for us we didn't know about.

The beautiful thing about trusting God in transition is God has grace that operates in the unknowns. His grace covers our failures, our mistakes, and our setbacks. When we decide to trust, God makes grace available to us that moves us forward even when we don't know how to make the right next move. This is why trusting God is the most critical of all transition decisions. Placing our faith, trust, and hope in an all-loving, all-knowing, and almighty God frees us from the pressure of trying to be perfect. Instead of living with the constant anxiety of trying to get things right, we can simply show up, knowing that the future is secured by God's grace.

Just Trust God

Every day, people around the world are busy making plans for their lives, preparing for what they think will be their futures. Every second, millions of people make decisions about everything from what to eat, what to wear, where to live, and who to marry. As early as we can talk, we're taught to think about what we will do with our lives. Teachers ask us, "What do you want to be when you grow up?" Doctor, lawyer, fireman—it made total sense to us then.

As we grew older, we realized we weren't good at math, so we stopped trying to be teachers. We realized we fainted at the sight of blood, so we couldn't be doctors. Then, we discovered things we liked and were interested in like music and arts. We thought we could do those things, but as we prepared for college, our advisors told us we couldn't build meaningful careers with those majors. Somewhere along the line in our 20s, reality started to set in. Some of the hope and optimism about what *could be* turned into anxiety, and we began to feel the pressure of needing to make serious plans for our future.

At this point, many of us began serious relationships, got married, had children, and started families. We embraced careers that allowed us to repay student loan debt and pay for the newfound obligations of our more firmly anchored lives. Suddenly, we go from being encouraged to make plans for our lives to feeling insecure, uncertain, and hesitant about the plans we have made, particularly when the unexpected changes of life alter those plans. While outwardly we seem to be doing well, inwardly, we are tormented by a litany of questions:

What if I chose the wrong career? The wrong relationship? The wrong major?

Should I have taken that other job offer?

What if I regret this path I'm on?

What if the plans I have for my life don't work out?

The trouble with planning our life is that we make plans with limited information and assumptions. We don't know what will happen in the future. We don't always know the motives and intentions of others. We can't always see ahead to changes in our industry that will cause corporations to lose money and lay off staff. We can't see that our spouses will be unfaithful and betray our trust. We can't see that sickness or sudden death will bring our happiness and sense of safety to a grinding halt.

Because we don't know, we often make decisions that impact our lives in ways we might one day regret. How many of you bought homes before the housing crisis? Don't you wish you had known that? How many of you have experienced bad relationships? Don't you wish you had known that before you said yes to the date? How many of us have had a job we hated? Wouldn't it have been great to know that before filling out the application?

We can't see the future. Whenever we make plans, we are really planning in the dark. We often set ourselves up for disappointment by planning around questions we cannot answer.

Will we be happy?

Will we succeed (whatever that means)?

Will we be safe?

Will we be OK?

The pressure of planning weighs heavily on our souls. Because we have planned our life out so much, we begin to equate our plan with our life, so much so our life becomes a slave to it. We teach ourselves to think if OUR PLAN isn't working, then OUR LIFE isn't working. If OUR PLAN is flawed, then OUR LIFE is flawed. If OUR PLAN fails, then OUR LIFE has failed.

But what if we've been thinking about this all the wrong way? What if our life doesn't need our plan? What if our hopes and dreams don't require the stress and strain of planning in the dark in order to be fulfilled? If this were true, we would be truly free to live. We wouldn't be under the pressure of wondering if the choices we're making are the right ones; we wouldn't be afraid of messing up or afraid of failure or of regrets. We would know everything is already OK, and we don't need any of our plans to work out, because we are trusting our lives to God's plan.

> *There are many plans in a man's heart, but it*
> *is the Lord's plan that will stand.*
> —Proverbs 19:21 (NLV)

I think it is oversimplified and misses the point to say God has a plan for my life. I think the better way to think about it is God has a plan, and He has already worked our lives into His plan. God's plan can be trusted because God knows the future. He knows the end from the beginning. He knows the outcome of every choice. HE KNOWS.

Any plan God has, God has infinite resources to back up. Our plans can fail sometimes because we don't always have what we need to make our plans happen. That is never God's problem.

God's plan can be trusted because His plan is to prosper us or move us forward. In other words, there is a goal in mind, and when we access God's plan for our life, it will never leave us in the same place. Progress is God's idea, and God's plan is to move us forward even after we have made decisions that work against our best interests because God already knew the choices we would make and every resulting outcome.

God's plan can be trusted because His plan is not to harm us. You and I have made some pretty dumb choices that have harmed us. God's plan will not harm us. You might say, "Well, I've had some pretty hurtful things happen to me—why is that? If God's plan is not to harm me, then why have I experienced so many tragedies, sicknesses, and disappointments beyond my control? Why is there even suffering in the world at all if His plan is not to harm me?"

These questions fail to consider two realities in their construction. First, suffering was NEVER part of God's original plan for humankind. Suffering in the world is the result of sin. Despite the reality of suffering, however, the Lord sovereignly repurposes the pain of suffering to form His identity in us and to reveal His character to us. Second, God's plan does not *harm*, even if it may often *hurt*. If two women approached me with a knife and announced they were going to cut me, and if I said yes to one and called the police on the other, what would be the difference? Likely, one would be a thief, seeking to do harm and take something from me that does not belong to her, while the other could be a surgeon, seeking to cause some hurt that might provoke healing by removing something from my body that does not belong there. The differentiating factor in how I respond to the two types of hurt is TRUST. I trust even though the surgeon WILL hurt me, the hurt will bring healing and not harm, so I will knowingly submit to the expectation of the pain because I trust its *purpose*.

Even in painful moments of change, the Lord's plan can be trusted. His plan takes into account the good and the bad, because all things work together for the good of those who love Him and are called according to His purpose (Romans 8:28). We might not always know how, but they do. The truth is that trusting the plan of God doesn't mean you will always avoid pain, but it does mean your pain will always have purpose. Any pain God allows as part of His plan will be used to work out a greater purpose in our lives.

God's plan can be trusted because God knows the future we hope for deep down in our hearts. In the deepest recesses of our soul, we each carry a code we've been born with, and that code is the hope of our life—the way that we are all born into the world. We are also, however, born with a nature that actually works against that hope in every way possible. It's called our sin nature. Our world has been altered in such a way that evil forces work against us from the time we are born to keep us from being who we really are. But God knows who we really are because He created each one of us, and He's so incredible that He knew us even BEFORE we were born. He loves us so much; He wants us to have every chance possible to be who we were created to be and discover the future He has planned for our lives.

Discovering the plan can only happen when you come into relationship with God. I'm not talking about "going to church" or "not going to hell." I'm not talking about habitual, predictable, and religious experiences. I'm talking about that which is core to the gospel, which is that God loves us so much and wants to set us free from the tyranny of our mistakes, our failures, our disastrous planning, and all other things that constitute our sinfulness so we can experience a more full, compelling, and complete connection with God—a connection that frees us from the crazy life of trying to make things happen for ourselves so we can be free to live in the moment, trusting God with our future, and being free to live without fear of success OR failure.

There is much talk today about *destiny:* the eventual, final outcome of our lives—the full picture of our future. We're taught to believe if we plan right, we can control our destiny. While our lives are greatly influenced by our decisions, our decisions do not control our destiny. We are free, then, from making decisions in transition that decide our future. It's not so much that our decisions shape our future—our decisions allow us to show up in the present.

Jerry Sittser devotes an entire chapter of his book *The Will of God as a Way of Life* to decision-making. In it, he writes:

> "We don't always know how our decisions will work out, but we know that God will work them out for our redemption. We will fall in love, change jobs, bury loved ones, say good-bye to children, move to faraway cities, raise cats, lose a fortune on the stock market, and end up living in Singapore. Sometimes we will make good decisions; sometimes not. Still, somehow God will work things out for our good, both because that is his nature and because that is his will for our lives."

Think about the last sneak preview you saw for a movie. Perhaps it was a commercial aired during your favorite TV show, or a short clip viewed on social media. Movie previews range from 15 seconds to about two minutes or so. There is a reason why commercials for movies are called sneak previews. There is a reason why these advertisements don't show an hour's worth of content. Sneak previews are intended to give you just enough content to compel you to show up. Sometimes, transition works the same way. You may not know exactly what the next scene of your life will unfold. Sometimes, life will provide you with unexpected plot twists.

And when this happens, we are tempted to think if we can't find a way to know how everything will turn out, it will somehow be the end of the world. When have we ever been watching a movie and come to the twisty, nail-biting, cliffhanger moment and turned to someone who has seen the movie before to ask for the spoiler? We don't normally do that because as anxious as those scenes in the movie make us, if someone tells us everything that will happen next, we somehow feel cheated. The truth is that no matter how concerned, curious, or panicky we become, we know allowing the drama to play out is just as satisfying as watching the conclusion. Our presence in the theater is proof we trust the director to resolve all the tension of those scenes when the movie ends. We know there is nothing for us to do except to sit back, relax, and watch until the end.

Perhaps you are facing a moment of transition in which life has handed you a plot twist. Perhaps characters in your life have developed more, and it has been revealed their intentions toward you are not as you had believed in the beginning. Perhaps your story is moving in a direction you could never have imagined, and depending upon the agent of change, perhaps that has brought you to an anxious excitement or an unknowing despair. You may be preparing to embrace an opportunity for which you had believed you were unqualified and have no idea what will be required of you to be successful in your role. Or perhaps you have received a terminal diagnosis, and while you are prepared to hope against hope, you are struggling with the thought of your life ending too soon.

In these transitions, there may be no grand decisions to be made. There may be no life-altering actions to be taken, or perhaps there might be, but the way forward seems completely out of your ability to grasp. There may be mysteries, but no trail of clues to help you solve them. We may pray feverishly for spoilers, and none will be found. We learn we cannot rewind, fast-forward, or change the channel. We learn life offers us far more peace when we can differentiate the transitions that demand our response from the transitions that compel us to simply show up, rest, and watch until the end.

CHAPTER 6:
DECIDE TO TELL

"You intended to harm me, but God intended it all for good. He brought me to this position so I could save the lives of many people."
—Genesis 50:20 (NLT)

One of my favorite things to do is to tell stories about the antics of my two-year-old daughter, Sage Olivia. She is growing into a beautiful, cheerful, and audacious young lady who will clearly lead one day, as she has no problem giving orders to everyone around. I actually had to upgrade my smartphone because I have more than 1,000 pictures and videos that chronicle our many moments together.

It's interesting, because I think we take for granted that we live in a moment in time where literally dozens of pictures can be taken, shared, posted—even edited—almost instantly with one swipe or touch to the screen of a smartphone. It wasn't always that way.

When I was a kid, cameras were not built into small, multitasking mobile phones. They were large devices about the size of a lunchbox that could not be carried around in large purses or suitcases. They were stored very carefully and only taken out for special events. They required batteries, flash cards, and rolls of film. Often, each roll of film only provided you with the opportunity to take 24 pictures—so if you were going on a trip, you either had to purchase plenty of film or choose your moments carefully!

When we finished taking pictures, we would remove the film rolls from the camera and take them to the local drug store, who would send them to a developer.

The developer would take the film to a dark room where there would be just enough light for her to see. Once in the dark room, she would open the film roll to expose the negatives and allow them to go through a process of developing. Once the images on the film were fully developed from the negatives, the photographs would be sent back to the drug store in an envelope that also contained the original negatives. It wasn't as convenient as it is now, but there was a sense of wonder and excitement about going to pick up your envelope to see what developed from the negatives.

Many of us have experienced negative changes in life. We have seen some dark moments, where life was especially difficult and discouraging. The good news is no matter how negative our experiences, transition gives us an opportunity to see what God can *develop from the negatives.*

Learning How to Tell Your Story

When we look at the life of Joseph in the Bible, we see one of the most incredible life stories in all of Scripture and an amazing account of God's power to develop the negatives. Starting in Genesis 37, we learn Joseph was favored by his father, Jacob. His father made a beautiful coat for him to wear as a symbol of that favor. We also learn this was one of the reasons why his brothers were deeply jealous of him. In addition, Joseph had two dreams, and in each dream, his relatives were all bowing down to him. Because of the special favor Joseph held with Jacob and the dreams Joseph shared, his brothers grew angry with him. They plotted to get rid of him. Joseph's story started off on a good note, but things seemingly began to take a negative turn.

Joseph was rejected by his brothers. As a matter of fact, they conspired among themselves and said, "Let's kill him —then we'll see what becomes of his dreams."

Joseph was betrayed and abandoned by the people closest to him.

He was lied on by people he served faithfully.

He was arrested for doing the right thing in a rough situation.

He was sent to prison after being wrongly convicted of a crime he didn't commit.

And in prison, he was forgotten by people who had promised to help him.

Perhaps you can relate to some of the changes Joseph experienced in transition. Maybe you have experienced the pain of being rejected by people close to you.

Perhaps you know the pain of having people be envious of you when you hoped that they would celebrate with you.

Maybe you have been falsely accused of things, and those accusations have caused major distress and delay in your life.

Perhaps you know what it feels like to be neglected, abandoned, and forgotten by people who promised to be there for you when you really need them.

If you have shared any of those experiences, then you may understand just how difficult transition was for Joseph as he navigated these painful twists and turns. If someone asks you to tell your story, you might be tempted to speak out of bitterness. You might be compelled to focus on what went wrong, how people let you down, and how people failed you. You might be tempted to say life has been unfair to you. If you shared any of those experiences with Joseph, you might be perfectly justified in doing so.

But near the end of Joseph's story, after he had been rejected by his brothers, thrown into a pit, sold into slavery, wrongly accused of sexual assault, and sent to prison and forgotten, Joseph had an opportunity to tell his story differently.

In Genesis 50, we see the same brothers who betrayed and abandoned Joseph were now fearful Joseph might one day take vengeance out on them:

> *After Jacob died, Joseph's brothers said to each other, "What if Joseph still hates us and wants to get even with us for all the cruel things we did to him?"*
> —Genesis 50:15 (CEV)

So, they humbly went to Joseph to beg his forgiveness. Joseph wept and told them, *"Don't be afraid! I have no right to change what God has decided. You tried to harm me …"*

Joseph acknowledged what was true. His brothers had tried to harm him. They were jealous of Joseph's favor with their father, Jacob, and they were offended by Joseph's dreams of a future in which his brothers would bow before him. Their envy became so wicked that they contemplated killing him and decided instead to abandon him in a pit. This traumatic experience led to a series of painful and discouraging moments in Joseph's life. With ultimate irony, their actions caused Joseph's dream to be fulfilled. They were now bowing before him, and he had the authority and opportunity to get revenge.

But instead of seeking vengeance, through his tears, Joseph forgave them with these words:

> *"But God made it turn out for the best, so that He could save all these people, as He is now doing. Don't be afraid! I will take care of you and your children."*
> —Genesis 50:19-21 (CEV)

After such a traumatic story, could you find the strength to speak those words?

How could Joseph look back on all of the painful changes he had experienced and reach THIS conclusion? Joseph's life unfolded centuries before any of the New Testament was written, so he didn't know about Romans 8:28 (NASB): "And we know that all things work together for the good of those who love God, to those who are the called according to His purpose." So how in the world could Joseph, after all he had been through, make this incredibly redemptive statement?

I believe in spite of all of the changes and challenges of Joseph's life, Joseph had learned how to tell his story, and not only that, he was able to locate the telling of his story within the context of a bigger picture. *"... God made it turn out for the best ... so that He could save all of these people, as He is now doing."* Joseph realized both the pain and the promise of his story were bigger than he thought. When he located his transition story in *context*, he was able to tell it with *confidence*.

It's Bigger Than You Think ...

All of us have a story; all of us have some memories that we will never forget, and all of us have been through some things we wish we could forget. Have you ever sat back and thought about the stuff you've gone through—good and bad—and asked yourself, *What does it all mean?* It's because we are taught that every story has a point. Whenever someone writes a book, a movie, a fable, or a story, they want us to see a main idea, a theme in the text, and they want to influence us to reach a conclusion based on the story.

What was the theme of Joseph's story? What helped him to make such a redemptive statement after all he had experienced in his life?

There is a phrase that continues to repeat itself in every painful moment of Joseph's story: "The Lord was with him."

The Lord was with Joseph when he was a slave in Potiphar's house, causing him to succeed in whatever he did (Genesis 39:2).

The Lord was with Joseph when he was wrongly accused and sent to prison, causing him to gain favor and influence there (Genesis 39:23).

The Lord was with Joseph when Pharaoh recognized his wisdom and favor with God and appointed him governor in Egypt (Genesis 41: 39-40).

Joseph had experienced many painful and disheartening changes. But in every situation, what helped Joseph to TRANSITION was the fact that through it all, *the Lord was with Him,* giving him favor, wisdom, and success. It was God's presence with Joseph that caused him to develop through every negative experience. Because God was with him, Joseph was able to look back over his life and realize even though he had experienced rejection, betrayal, abandonment, oppression, accusation, and neglect, God was at work in every transition, using every negative experience to develop him into the person God had created him to be. When given the opportunity to do otherwise, Joseph instead looked into the eyes of the very people who had harmed him and decided to tell his story.

What has helped me to reconcile every moment of transition I have experienced in life is the ability to tell my story. The good, the bad, and the ugly. I find that the more I mature, the more I can tell. I can unpack the pain of losing loved ones because though I may not have all of the information (God, why did this happen?), I can tell the story of my TRANSFORMATION. (Here's how God used this experience to develop me.)

When I'm able to tell my story, it reminds me change is not the enemy. Loss is not the enemy. Pain and suffering are not the enemy. The worst thing that could possibly happen to me (in life) is for me to *lose the awareness of who God is and who I am becoming.* Telling my story helps me to see God's power at work in every moment of pain and reminds me that *pain is never purposeless.* It reminds me there is a hidden treasure of wisdom tucked away in every experience, and often, *the dirtier the transition, the greater the treasure.*

Unless you've skimmed this book, you've realized by now in almost every chapter, I tell a part of my own story. It is not because I wanted the challenge of writing a book that was both instructive as well as autobiographical. It was not because I didn't have access to the stories of others. And while I think I have led an interesting life, I'm not arrogant enough to think that you should find my story more fascinating than others. The decision to tell my story throughout the pages of this book was very intentional.

I have learned the best stories, whether in print or on screen, are not the ones where our focus is upon the events of the narrative. I have learned the best stories, the stories we remember, watch over and over again, and share with others, are the ones where we are able to see the way characters change as the story unfolds. While entertaining, what made *Forrest Gump* a great movie is not the fact he became rich by owning a shrimp boat or that he met three presidents in his lifetime. What made the movie great was we got to see the story of a simple man who lived an incredible life, but his most poignant and powerful moments of growth happened in the simple things of life we all can relate to: love, friendship, family, and understanding the meaning of life. We see a lovable character navigate incredible moments of transition to arrive at a place in life where he was able to distill those experiences, filled with joy and sorrow, into wisdom that allowed him to more fully come alive right before our eyes. Without this nuance, you have a film that could have easily been forgotten among thousands. It is the telling of a person's story—specifically the transformation that occurs as a result of their story—that causes us to lean in and absorb insight that can be applied to our wider narrative.

Sometimes, change brings such a level of difficulty to our lives that we can feel like we are alone in a story. The truth is that we all belong to an incredible epic story—a metanarrative that encompasses the compelling stories of trillions of people who have lived and are yet alive. Every time we decide to share our story, we remind ourselves we are not alone, especially in the transitions. We are not the only ones who have had to make difficult decisions to leave familiar situations. We are not the only ones grieving seemingly insurmountable losses. We are not the only ones traversing through time, sometimes confidently and many times with great uncertainty. *We are not alone in our changes. We are not alone in our transitions.*

I did not want to write a sterile, distant book of transition policies and procedures. I wanted to share my story and the lessons I have learned. I wanted someone to read this book and not only discover how to get unstuck, but to know there's someone who knows what being stuck feels like. I wanted someone to read this book and not only learn how to dream a new dream but also realize there are others who know what it feels like to have to let a dream go and consider trusting a future that promises you nothing.

I wanted to tell my story because the decision to TELL is a decision that reminds us that our transitions are not just about us. It reminds us there is someone else who needs the clarity, the hope, the assurance, the motivation, the empathy, and the resolve that help us to move forward. It is a reminder when we are tempted to be more self-centered and self-focused than is healthy, that this does not help us to transition; it actually disrupts our forward movement because our desire to share our lives with others is the strong chain that keeps us connected to the larger story. As long as we can remain connected to the bigger picture, we will always have access to the power of transition.

The weird, invisible, immeasurable essence of transition power flows through relationships. It flows when we are able to see just how much our lives matter to the bigger picture. It flows when we realize our pain can serve a purpose. It flows when we realize somewhere, someone needs the truth we've learned, the strength we've gained, the hope we've held onto, and the faith that held us together when we almost fell apart. It flows when we realize *we won't* change *change until* change changes *us and* changes *our ability to bring meaningful* change *to others.*

May we always see how our transition decisions fit into the greater story. May our decisions shape and form us into people who bring hope, change, and solutions to the world. *May we never be so selfish to think our problems are all about us.* Instead, may we see every difficulty as an opportunity to receive wisdom that can be shared with others. May we see every transition we experience in life as a chance to ask, "Whose lives are impacted by the decisions I make?"

Our transitions create a story. They tell a story of what we have experienced, who we have become, and why it matters. Our stories are a gift. Our stories help us know how we are called to serve others. God uses two pens to write our stories: His love and our decisions.

When You See Me, You've Seen My Decisions …

> "When we're born, we look like our parents …
> when we die, we look like our decisions."
> —Bishop Dale Bronner

Anyone who has ever seen a picture of me next to Catherine Marshall knows it would be hard to argue she isn't my mother. When you see me, you've seen her.

When you see me, you've also seen my decisions.

I've experienced many changes over the course of my life: growth, death, marriage, parenting, relocation, miracles, betrayal, promotions, and more. Throughout these experiences, I have made decisions—some I celebrate, and some I lament. Each of these decisions has developed me into the man I am today. As I reflect on all of my transitions, there is no denying it—I look like my mother, but I also look like my decisions.

However, now I am able to tell the story because, through my story, I now know something critically important about decisions.

Each day that you wake up and look in the mirror, there is a chance one day you will realize something: While you cannot change the decisions you've made or the path you've traveled, you will realize you're not finished, and you are STILL becoming. Suddenly, your decisions will carry more weight. When that day comes, you may grow more generous with your money and less frivolous with your time. You will become more confident about your YES and less hesitant (and less apologetic) about your NO.

When that day comes, you will look back over the joys and pains of every transition, and a deep gratitude will flood your soul. You will realize several things: All of your experiences were instructive. You've made mistakes, but you don't have to repeat them. You've lost some things and some people, but the fact that you MISS THEM means that you were blessed to HAVE HAD THEM. And neither your ignorance nor your brilliance has ever been or will ever be greater than God's sovereignty and His mercy. You will feel less regretful over your past and more resolute concerning your future.

On that day, a significant part of your existential fog will clear. Your priorities will be evident. You will live with greater peace, clarity, passion, and intention than ever before. On that day, you will no longer see change as an enemy, but as an agency of transition, creating opportunities for you to be who God created you to be, do what God created you to do, and live the life God created you to live. No matter what changes you face and how long it takes, you will eventually realize exactly how to respond *in THAT moment* and *make your NEXT move*.

May TODAY be THAT DAY for you.

ACKNOWLEDGMENTS

*To my wife, Veronica, and daughter, Sage.
Thank you for the ample supply of grace
that allowed me to finish this book.*

*To CheRhonda Greenlee, Lynda Randolph,
and the entire team for their invaluable
support in helping me cross the finish line.*

www.ingramcontent.com/pod-product-compliance
Lightning Source LLC
Chambersburg PA
CBHW051950090625
27926CB00017B/763